CISTERCIAN FATHERS SERIES: NUMBER TWENTY-SIX

GILBERT OF HOYLAND

Volume Three

ON THE
SONG OF SONGS

THE WORKS OF
GILBERT *of* HOYLAND

Translated and introduced by
LAWRENCE C. BRACELAND SJ

CISTERCIAN FATHERS SERIES: NUMBER TWENTY-SIX

Sermons on the Song of Songs, III

α
Cistercian Publications
www.cistercianpublications.org

LITURGICAL PRESS
Collegeville, Minnesota
www.litpress.org

A Cistercian Publications title published by Liturgical Press

Cistercian Publications
Editorial Offices
161 Grosvenor Street
Athens, Ohio 45701
www.cistercianpublications.org

This book has been published with the help of a grant from the Canadian Federation for the Humanities, using funds provided by the Social Sciences and Humanities Research Council of Canada.

The translation here presented is based on the edition of Jean Mabillon, Milan, Gnocchi, reprint of 1852.

Original Latin title:
Sermones in Canticum Salomonis ab eo loco ubi B. Bernardus morte praeventus desiit.

The Gnocchi reprint of 1852 has been checked against the Migne reprint of 1854, *Patres Latini* 184. Discrepancies between the two reprints were checked against microfilm copies of twelfth century manuscripts: Paris, Bibliothèque National, 9605 and 8546; Bruges, Stadsbibliotheek, 49; Madrid, Bibliotheca Nacional 512. Our sincere thanks to the librarians.

© Cistercian Publications, Inc., 1979

Available in Europe and the Commonwealth from
A. R. Mowbray & Co Ltd.
Saint Thomas House Becket Street
Oxford OX1 1SG England

Ecclesiastical permission to publish this work has been granted by Bernard Flanagan, Bishop of Worcester.

ISBN 978-0-87907-126-4

TO FOLLOWERS OF THE RULE OF SAINT BENEDICT

Hinc celer egrediens facili, mea carta, volatu
per silvas, colles, valles quoque prepete cursu
alma deo cari Benedicti tecta require.
Est nam certa quies fessis venientibus illuc,
hic olus hospitibus, piscis hic, panis abundans;
pax pia, mens humilis, pulcra et concordia fratrum,
laus, amor et cultus Christi simul omnibus horis.

Across the hills and in the valley's shade,
    Alone the small script goes,
Seeking for Benedict's beloved roof,
    Where waits its sure repose.
They come and find, the tired travellers,
    Green herbs and ample bread,
Quiet and brothers' love and humbleness,
    Christ's peace on every head.

        translation by Helen Waddell, *Mediaeval Latin Lyrics*

CONTENTS

SERMON 33	*Spirit, Power, Mercy, and all Graces*	399
SERMON 34	*Works, lips, and spirit*	413
SERMON 35	*Fruits of the fountain and the garden*	425
SERMON 36	*The spices of all the virtues*	435
SERMON 37	*A well and a fountain, wisdom and love*	445
SERMON 38	*Wintry north and warm south winds*	457
SERMON 39	*Freedom, affectivity and grace*	467
SERMON 40	*Continence, repentance, and all virtues*	477
SERMON 41	*Milk, honey and wine*	491
SERMON 42	*Exchanging visits*	503
SERMON 43	*From action to contemplation*	515
SERMON 44	*Gone from the cloister*	527
SERMON 45	*Her mantle from the watchmen*	539
SERMON 46	*Languishing with love*	551
SERMON 47	*The beauty of the Nazarite*	559
SERMON 48	*Radiant with light, red with fire*	571
Mira Simplicitas		575
ABBREVIATIONS		597

Library of Congress Cataloging in Publication Data (Revised)

Gilbert, Abbot of Swineshead, Holland, Lincolnshire.
   Sermons on the Song of songs.

   (His The works of Gilbert of Hoyland; v. 1-)
(Cistercian fathers series : no. 14, 20, 26
   Bibliography:
   Includes index.
   1. Bible. O.T. Song of Solomon—Sermons.
I. Title. II. Series.
BS1485.G49   223'.9'066   77-23026
ISBN 0-87907-426-4

GILBERT OF HOYLAND

Volume Three

ON THE
SONG OF SONGS

SERMON 33
SPIRIT, POWER, MERCY, AND ALL GRACES

The bride is anointed with spirit, power, mercy, and all graces. 1. At Easter one should come to the tomb with spiritual ointments. 2. Anointing means a good conscience, fragrance a good reputation. 3. How ointments differ from perfume; the good works of virtue are insipid and displeasing without the unction of the Spirit. 4. How attractive is the unction of mercy! How ready Christ is to pardon! 5. Hope of mercy raises up the despondent; Christ's mercy is a model for pastors. 6. Ointments and ways of anointing are varied. 7-8. Ointments and their fragrance are distinguished. 9. Pride and tepidity make the prayer of the Pharisee malodorous.

THE FRAGRANCE OF YOUR OINTMENTS SURPASSES ALL PERFUMES.*[1]   Sg 4:10

This day of the Lord's Resurrection which we solemnly celebrate each year compels me to begin my sermon by returning to our discussion of the ointments. Today the women come with perfumes.* Nicodemus likewise comes 'bearing a mixture of myrrh and aloes weighing about a hundred pounds'.* Mary Magdalen herself 'anointed the body' of Jesus 'in anticipation of his burial'.* You see what important mysteries are celebrated in ointments. They are great mysteries and who is qualified to discuss them? Who will worthily discern

Mk 16:1

Jn 19:39
Mk 14:8. Miquel 154, n. 15.

the differences between the ointments and expound their properties? Deliberation on this subject requires a man of experience, not of opinions. Indeed it is not easy for anyone to discuss these ointments unless his teacher has been Unction in person.

Today the Lord was anointed 'with the oil of gladness more than his fellows,'* yet not without his fellows. For how does one share as a fellow, who does not rejoice and make glad and does not rise to new joy together with him who rises? This is indeed an opportune time to discuss the ointments with you, but a time much more opportune to be filled with the fragrance of ointments. You demand a sermon of me and I ask of you the fragrance of ointments. By what right do you haunt the tomb of the Lord Jesus with the holy women, if you bring to it no spiritual ointment? Today the Lord's flesh was gloriously changed thanks to the oil.* Does it not seem fitting that our hearts should be changed and transformed into the oil of the spirit, the oil of exultation and gladness?*

I had begun a sermon about ointments and here our discussion bogs down in oil. Now what has oil to do with ointment? Not a little, and if oil is not the same in every respect, oil approaches and resembles ointment to some extent. For although oil is not fragrant, it soothes; oil does not smell sweet but you are well anointed with oil. Here however the Bridegroom extols not so much the unction as the fragrance in the ointments of the bride. 'And the fragrance of your ointments', he says, 'surpasses all perfume.'

2. Not every soul abounds in sweet-smelling ointments, as that woman in the book of Kings says to the prophet: there is 'in my house only a little oil to anoint myself'.* This woman has no ointments compounded of sweet-smelling spices but a little plain oil for anointing. Mary Magdalen, a woman not of the Law but of the Gospel, brings an ointment of precious spikenard, not a little but a whole pound.* And Simon himself is reproached by the Lord with not having anointed his head even with oil, while she poured ointment over his head.* Do you see how

ointments are preferred to oil, especially sweet-smelling ointments? For in addition to fulfilling their function of anointing, they anticipate it with some blessing of spiritual fragrance.

Ointment indeed is more limited but its fragrance circulates among many. Even though but one person be anointed, he is not the only one to share its bouquet. The bouquet of the ointment is shared by all, since it circulates among all. Therefore the anointing is yours; its fragrance belongs to others as well as to yourself. He is well anointed and fully fragrant, who enjoys blessings in God's sight and shares blessings in men's sight. 'Rejoice in the Lord always,' with Paul, 'and again I say rejoice; let your modesty be known to all men.'* Apply the joy to ointments, men's awareness of your modesty to its fragrance. Hear how Paul himself speaks of awareness as fragrance. 'And everywhere He manifests the fragrance of our awareness of Him.'* *Ph 4:4-5*

2 Co 2:14

Good then is the ointment and good is its fragrance, spiritual exultation in the Lord and its modest manifestation, happiness and awareness. He is well anointed whom the Lord delights in the happiness of his inner conscience and who is delighted in the Lord; and his fragrance is sweet who with Paul delights all men in everything he does and delights them only in the Lord;* for in his modest demeanor, discreet labor and learned speech, the ointments of inward eagerness and grace yield their fragrance. He is well anointed who glories in the Lord and his fragrance is sweet through whom the Lord is glorified before men. To the man himself who yields the fragrance of the Lord, his own fragrance is sweet, if he does not boast that he himself is praised but that the Lord is praised through him.

1 Co 10:33.
Lam 18, n. 78.

3. 'The fragrance of your ointments surpasses all perfumes.' Do you wish me to suggest for you the difference between ointments and perfumes? Well does this very text of the Canticle seem to make the distinction not by depreciating perfumes but by preferring ointments. As far then as I can find any difference between similar and related substances,

ointments can be seen as gifts of grace conferred through the Holy Spirit,* while perfumes are our duties faithfully referred to the Holy Spirit.† In our tasks and duties exists the attractive beauty of natural goodness but in ointment exists the grace of the Spirit. You read that the Lord Jesus was 'anointed with spirit and virtue';* so also it was fitting that his bride should resemble him in this respect, that she also should be 'anointed with spirit and virtue'.

Good are the perfumes of the virtues and though they seem to have their own bouquet, they yield an aroma filled with more grace, when sprinkled with the 'fragrance of sweetness' from the unction of the Spirit.* The perfume of good works and virtues we can share in common with outsiders; ointments we cannot share in common. Scripturally, although virtues and good works are beautiful in themselves, they are more pleasing when they proceed from the Spirit. Why do men glorify God when they see good works, if not because they understand that the good work itself comes from God and returns to God?* Surely if there are any good works in me, they are more pleasing to me when they are ascribed to the grace of Christ,* when his unction in me is extolled and when the Spirit yields a sweet fragrance, than when my natural power of choice or the fruit of my industry is applauded.

Scripturally, without the unction of the Spirit nature is deprived of freedom, virtue of truth and work of merit.* For without the grace of the Spirit and faith in Christ, the effort of the will lacks effectiveness, what seems to be virtue is a veneer and the work does not reap a harvest of eternal reward. Therefore 'the fragrance of your ointments surpasses all perfumes'. For however varied their bouquet may be, these perfumes do not diffuse a fragrance of unadulterated sweetness, unless the anointing grace of the Spirit is diffused through them wave upon wave.

4. Do you wish me to set before you an ointment whose fragrance surpasses all other perfumes of the

Church's gifts? In the Church what fragrance breathes a sweeter scent than that of mercy and forgiveness? How many have run in the fragrance of this ointment and through it been incorporated and engrafted in Christ! Sweet is its scent as it destroys in a moment the stench of inveterate corruption and of sin long ingrained.

How malodorous was that woman who was in the city, Mary by name, as she approached the feet of Jesus in the house of Simon the leper! How she stank in the nostrils of Simon himself, who could not endure the loathsomeness of her presence. How she stank, I say, as she approached Jesus! Yet notice how the fragrance of her repentance and love and of the grace she received is spread through the world! The grace of Christ does not delay; at the very banquet at which this woman bathed, wiped and anointed the Lord's feet, she is washed and wiped clean and fully anointed and preferred to the Pharisee by the witness of the Lord himself.* For the clemency of Christ is neither niggardly nor indolent; it repays with interest and repays on the spot. What wonder if his pardon runs to meet the penitent, when his patience escorts her to repentance! Behold that woman taken in adultery and abandoned in the midst of all! Notice how she perfumed the air with the aroma of his clemency, though previously she reeked of the guilt of her wantonness.² *Lk 7:37-50*

Thumb through the Gospel; everywhere you will find Jesus both quick and spendthrift in pardon. In John, although a man has been dead four days and now stinks according to the sad news published about him, when Jesus summons and leads him from the tomb of bad habit, when Jesus unbinds him and applies the ointment of forgiveness, on the spot there vanishes from his countenance all the stench of aging corruption.* Who indeed will re-examine a charge not made by the Lord? Who will retain the errors which he remits?³ That cannot be fetid which he fills with fragrance. 'Lord', said Martha, 'he has been dead four days and by now he stinks.'* Yours is the error, Martha; Jesus does not take flight from *Jo 11:1-44*

Jo 11:39

what stinks, but rather sends the stench packing. He set the example for his Church, that as he did for us personally, so we also should do for one another.* These are the ointments he left to his Church.

5. How many in desperation would have given themselves up to all uncleanness and avarice,* and hurled themselves headlong into the whirlpool of all vices, if they had not been drawn back by the fragrance of this remedy! 'I would be distressed,' we chant, 'if I did not know the mercies of the Lord',[4] mercies in the Head and mercies in his Body which is the Church. For she also has received from the Lord what she hands on to her children.[5] She has received mercy in trust, I say, and in the command to her that she be the handmaid of mercies. Good it is to be mercy's servant, but better to be mercy's self.

The mercy you owe in virtue to your office, dispense from the heart. Manifest in yourself the affection of Christ whose office and place you have accepted. You are the minister of the One 'who is rich in mercy'.* Do not be found overharsh in what belongs to another. Distribute to your fellow servants[6] their measure of this ointment in good time. 'If you are unfaithful in what belongs to another, who will give you what is your own?'* Let your affection be one of mercy, for mercy is the result of the Lord's pardon. The man who nurses an injured conscience or a hidden wound[7] in his breast, will trust himself to you without anxiety if he scents in you the fragrance of this ointment. 'If you only knew what this means: "I desire mercy and not sacrifice", you would never have condemned the guiltless.'* Not so do you act, O Lord, not so! Not only do you not condemn the guiltless, but even the guilty you do not condemn but correct.

'The just man,' says the psalmist, 'shall correct me in mercy, but the oil of the wicked shall not anoint my head.'* Here the psalmist distinguishes between one oil and another, between the oil of flattery and the oil of mercy. The former soothes and wounds; the latter soothes and heals. Does not the ointment by which all sins are so easily blotted out have a sweeter fragrance for you than all perfumes? That younger son coming to his senses, even from a far off country, perceived the rich supply of this ointment in his father, and amid droves of hogs, the fragrance of his father's clemency began to perfume the air. So the son was allured and began to run to his father 'in the fragrance of his ointments'.* See how accessible, how overflowing is the grace of the Lord Jesus. He finds it fitting to rejoice and feast with the repentant son.* He stays in Zacchaeus' home;† he co-opts a tax gatherer as his disciple** and with Lazarus straight from the tomb he celebrates a feast.†† He cannot reproach those to whom he is propitious; he does not know how to confer a half-measure of clemency; those whom he forgives, he welcomes into his familiar friendship.⁸

Sg 1:3

*Lk 15:11-32
†Lk 19:1-10
**Mt 9:9; 10:3
††Jo 12:1-2

6. Good then is the ointment of mercy, because it forgives sins, because it anticipates, accompanies and accumulates merits. It surpasses the fragrance of all perfumes, because the whole assembly of the saints relies more on mercy than on merit. In James, the ointment of forgiveness is the last Sacrament.* This ointment is a blessing bestowed on sinner and saint alike. But some other ointments are reserved for the saints and suited to them alone. There are ointments which heal, ointments which strengthen, ointments which sanctify, ointments which give delight. The first dispel sickness; the second add zest to those who are already healthy; the third sanctify for the work of the ministry, as royal and priestly unctions sanctify; the fourth are intended not for work but for leisure; not for administration but for love, for glory, for delight, for the use of the Bridegroom and his bride.

Jm 4:14-15

It is good to linger among ointments, but since enough has been said elsewhere about their various kinds,* let us now briefly distinguish the various ways of anointing. Some persons are touched, others are sprinkled, others daubed, others steeped in ointments. Reread the Pentateuch, unroll the Gospel again and make moral applications of the various ways of anointing performed externally upon the

See Bernard, SC 10 ff.

body. I am now concerned not with the nature of the ointments but with the measure of the anointing. Some persons receive ointments once, others often, others all the time. Good is this frequency, provided grace is also present. Neither sweetness nor plenty seems to be lacking in the bride's ointments, for 'their fragrance surpasses all perfumes'.

7. We have applied this eulogy to the Church in general; let us now direct the sermon to some specific person in the Church, one who through some singular gift of love and familiarity should be graced with the name of 'bride', one in whom the ointments not only of kinship but also of worthiness and charm perfume the air with rich fragrance. In my opinion such a person has neither been touched in some part nor sprinkled here and there with the sacred unction, but more bountifully steeped and wholly anointed in the delights of the Bridegroom. In the palace of this Bridegroom, ample storerooms are filled with perfumes, overflowing from room to room as befits the wealth of kings. But it is not beyond belief that the queen diffuses the fragrance of more excellent ointments. Yet nothing is told us about the effectiveness of the ointments beyond the fact that only their fragrance is extolled. The Bridegroom does not mention the effect of the anointing, being content to recall only their delights and preferably those delights which enkindle spiritual love.

Anointing is felt only by the sense of touch, when oil has been poured upon the flesh. But fragrance, eluding the sense of touch, allows itself to be experienced only in breathing. And while ointment liquefying gradually seeps downwards, its fragrance mounts upward unhindered, infiltrates the brain and while it occupies the seat of the senses, brings refreshment. The fragrance therefore of the ointments is much finer and more subtle than their fluid. And in the bride's wooing, it was fitting to mention what is more delicate, more adapted to spiritual delights and less cloyed with sediment. Other persons need ointments and oil either to allay or to transform the movements of the flesh. But the bride, as becomes the betrothed of the Lord, is now filled not in the flesh but in the spirit with delights of the spirit. 'The fragrance of your ointments surpasses all perfumes.'

Although only fragrance is mentioned, perhaps fragrance does not operate alone but anointing co-operates. 'Those who belong to Christ,' says the apostle, 'have crucified their flesh with its passions and desires.'* Where there is anointing, crucifixion seems unnecessary. The latter brings death while the former brings change. Crucifixion indeed inflicts pain, but anointing alleviates pain. Unction is gentle though effective, for without injury, by the oil of exultation and gladness,* unction keeps the flesh unharmed from corruption, banishes decay and inflicts no torment. Ointments anticipate and ointments follow the Passion of the Lord Jesus, that you also may learn to allay any possible torments of your flesh by an outpouring of abundant ointments. Twice was the Lord anointed, that he might not feel the insult and injury of the Cross and might achieve the renewal of his Resurrection, and that by his sacrament, as it were, he might commend the grace of spiritual anointing. Good then is the ointment when its flow, so to speak, transforms the flesh and when its fragrance refreshes the spirit.

Ga 5:24

Ps 44:8; Hb 1:9

8. To sum up in brief: anointing is an exultation of the mind and its fragrance is prayer. Anointing is spiritual gladness and its fragrance is some exterior awareness by reputation of what takes place in the spirit. Anointing is inward delight and its fragrance is a desire flowing gently from joyful experience. Therefore 'the fragrance of your ointments surpasses all perfumes'. Indeed the incense of every other prayer and desire is surpassed in vehemence[9] by that longing which is born from the wooing of heavenly joy and from the ardor, which like a most enchanting fragrance, rises in abundance from the anointing of the Spirit. Good is this longing which has the power of prayer without the distress of affliction.

She is the bride to whom this privilege of ointment and fragrance is accorded. What wonder if hers is a more excellent fragrance, when hers is a more special anointing! What wonder if her hunger is keener, when she savors what is sweeter! For it is only right that she who clings more closely should pray more fully. Clinging to the Bridegroom, she has been made one spirit with him.* Wherefore only the Spirit yields his fragrance in her, for he has anointed her and prays for her with affections too deep for words.* Therefore 'the fragrance of her ointments surpasses all perfumes'. Again in the Apocalypse you read of 'bowls full of incense, which are the prayers of the saints'.* Perfumes, as Exodus teaches, are divided for two uses: namely for anointing and for the offering of incense.*

9. Do both these not seem to you to be combined now in the praise of the bride? Her ointments are not only ointments but also most odoriferous, for 'their fragrance surpasses all perfumes'. Ointment, as has been said, is the reception of gifts; fragrance is thanksgiving for their reception, desire for eternal gifts and a feeling of humility amid sublime blessings. For 'the prayer of the man who humbles himself penetrates even the clouds'.* Do you see how the incense of humble prayer ascends?

That Pharisee ascended into the Temple to pray but the fragrance of his prayer knew not how to ascend. He reviews for himself the gifts of graces granted him by God and, as it were, enumerates anointings. 'I am not', he says, 'like the rest of men, extortioners, unjust, adulterers.' Do you hear at whose expense he boasts that he has been anointed? His glory is in the confusion of others. Though not much to boast about, his glory seems much to him. It smells sweet to him though not 'above perfumes' but only above the nauseating fumes of 'the rest of men'.

You have heard to what his anointings are preferred; hear now the elements of grace which his ointments display, over which the Pharisee boasts: 'I fast twice a week, I give tithes of all I possess, and if I have cheated anyone I make fourfold restitution.'* These good works reek of the rudiments of the Law, not the perfection of the Gospel.[10] He does not fast at all times, he does not renounce all his possessions, so as to have nothing from which to give the firstfruits or the tithes. He makes fourfold restitution when he has defrauded others, but he does not allow himself to be defrauded, does not offer what is left to one who takes away a part, does not say he has endured wrongdoing.* *Lk 6:29-30*

O Pharisee, amid feeble deeds you are boastful beyond measure![11] O Pharisee, you do not invoke God, but invoke insults on the tax collector hard by! You bear witness concerning yourself; your witness counts for little. Two faults in your prayer yield not so much a fragrance as a stench: pride and lukewarmness. The pride consists in your reproaching the tax collector, the lukewarmness in your asking for nothing at all. For how shall a prayer not be lukewarm which is filled with the bombast and the hollowness of self-adulation? O Pharisee, you do not praise God; you praise yourself! You bear witness concerning yourself and your witness is not true.* *Jo 5:31* The evidence for your good work is slight; the evidence for preferring yourself to others is false.

Now listen to the witness of Truth: 'I tell you solemnly, the publican went down to his house justified rather than the other.'*[12] 'For it is not the man who commends himself who is accepted but the man whom the Lord commends.'* Happy then is the soul for which such an excellent recommendation is given by Truth itself: 'The fragrance of your ointments surpasses all perfumes.' Great as was the evidence given for the tax collector, much greater witness is given to the bride for whom is sung the eulogy of our text. 'That man went down to his house justified rather than the Pharisee', that is rather than the proud man, the unjust man, but 'the fragrance of the bride's ointments surpasses all perfumes'. Here is a noble encomium, but she does not hear the witness of a man but of the One who searches hearts,* who by faith and love both dwells and works in her heart. She does not commend herself; she does not reproach others. Indeed 'her lips are a dripping honeycomb'.* This verse comes

Lk 18:14

2 Co 10:18

Rv 2:23

Sg 4:11

next but it cannot be dealt with today. Tomorrow's discourse will give your hearing and your eagerness, joy and gladness in the Lord Jesus. This may He grant who lives and reigns for ever and ever. Amen.

NOTES ON SERMON THIRTY-THREE

1. G. writes to one individual, except in par. 1, the second sentence of par. 3 and the first sentence of par. 4.
2. Jn 8:3-11. Lam 7, n. 14; 180, n. 63; for *evangelium revolve,* S 33:6, 34:1.
3. Often G.'s reflections are redolent of the Prayers of St Anselm; Anselm asks, 'who will make excuse for him whom God accuses?' (Ward, 142, 1. 45) Here G. asks antiphonally: 'Who will re-examine a charge not made by the Lord? Who will retain the errors which he remits?' The originals show a closer link in sentence structure.
4. In the Cistercian and Roman Breviaries, this is the responsory to lesson VII, nocturn II of Vigils for the First Sunday of Lent.
5. 1 Co 11:23. See A. Ampe, 'Exemplarisme,' DSp 4 (1961) 1877.
6. Reading *conservis* with mss Paris 9605, 8546, Bruges 49, Madrid 512, Mab, for *conversis* of Migne.
7. Reading *caecum* of Paris 9605, 8546, Bruges 49, Madrid 512, for *tectum* of Mab. and Migne.
8. On *familiaritas,* see S 33:5, 7; 44:2; 45:3; 46:3; Lam 187, n. 114.
9. Reading *vehementiam* with mss Paris 9605, 8546, Bruges 49, Madrid 512, Migne, for *vehementia* of Mab. On the joy of experience see Miquel 157-8, n. 28; Lam 192, n. 149.
10. Reading *perfectionem* with mss Paris 9605, 8546, Bruges 49, Troyes 917, for *doctrinam* of Madrid 512, Mab. and Migne.
11. With mss Paris 9605, 8546, Bruges 49, Madrid 512, Troyes 917, Mab. and Migne reading *infirma* rather than the suggested *infima.*
12. G. begins his quotation with 'Amen, Amen' as if from Jn.

SERMON 34
WORKS, LIPS AND SPIRIT

The bride pleases in works, lips and spirit. 1. From the Bridegroom through the Spirit comes the rank of ministry and the grace to minister. 2. The bride's lips are compared to a honeycomb because they distill the sweetness of the fourfold works of his word. 3. Sweet is her pardon and her prayer. 4. Her lips are a honeycomb thanks to the kiss of charity and the utterance of truth. 5. She distills the honey of mysteries and pours with discretion the milk of consolation. 6. Her cloak of strength is in fasting and incense is in her prayer. 7. The garment of good deeds and the raiment of the flesh lend charm to her body and win grace for her soul. 8. The bride pleases her Bridegroom in words, works, and the Spirit.

YOUR LIPS ARE A DRIPPING HONEYCOMB, MY BRIDE: HONEY AND MILK ARE BENEATH YOUR TONGUE: THE FRAGRANCE OF YOUR GARMENTS IS LIKE THE FRAGRANCE OF INCENSE*[1]   *Sg 4:11*

Passionately tender are the words now addressed to the bride. But you ask how they relate to what precedes. Once should have been enough to remind you that the law of eulogy is free from the obligation of logical sequence.* It does not follow a chain but enjoys freedom to wander. Where the logic of praise is concerned, order cannot indeed be demanded, but it   *G. S 1:1* should not be brushed aside if it can be identified. Immediately after the eulogy of ointments, the grace of her lips is introduced. Have you any reason to doubt that through the power of the ointment this grace was diffused upon her lips?* Consult the Gospel and you will find a similar remark about the Bridegroom himself: 'The Spirit of the Lord,' he says, 'is upon me, because he has anointed me; he sent me to preach good news to the poor.'*

Fittingly the bride was likened to the Bridegroom, in being also anointed for the work of the Gospel by the unction of the Spirit. For the Spirit anoints both for office and for effectiveness. Both come from him: the rank of ministry and the grace to minister. Without grace the rank is useless and without rank the exercise of grace is presumptuous. 'How shall they preach, if they are not sent, unless they are anointed?'* As it was written, 'The Spirit of the Lord . . . has anointed me; he has sent me to preach good news to the poor.'* The Spirit ordains to office. The Spirit both opens the mouth and teaches it to speak. Therefore in the eulogy of the bride, the Bridegroom deals first with ointments and then with the sweetness of her lips, for although she utters a gentle message, she is not the speaker, but the Spirit of the Bridegroom speaks in her. In the Gospel, listen to what the Bridegroom himself, Jesus, promises to his pristine bride, that is, to the apostles who received the firstfruits of the Spirit: 'I will give you a mouth and wisdom,' he says, 'which none of your adversaries will be able to withstand or contradict.* Great indeed is the power of God's word; it can both refute adversaries and win those who are not adversaries.

Now the Lord's promise concerns the preaching of the word; but what is central to our discussion, his promise, looks more to persuasion than to the effectiveness of refutation: 'Your lips are a dripping honeycomb.' It is a family trait and, as it were, inborn in her to speak sweetly. But if ever she gives a severe rebuke it is foreign to her, imported from afar and not inherent in her; if she rebukes, it is not from disposition but under duress. When she speaks sweetly, she speaks in character, but when harshly, what provokes her is not the temper of her tongue but the distemper of her audience. Therefore, for what is a family trait and in character, the Bridegroom praises her in the words: 'Your lips are a dripping honeycomb.'

2. Since you have now heard something about the link with what precedes, do you wish me to expand upon the content of this eulogy? The eulogy contains three points: sweetness, fulness, and thrift. The sweetness of the honeycomb is considered in its quality, fulness in its abundance, thrift in its outpouring. Why do I say outpouring? It is rather a distillation than an outpouring, for 'your lips are a dripping honeycomb'. Why need we linger to give each point its application? You know yourselves that a honeycomb pours out only sweetness and pours sweetness only from a full comb and indeed pours some but not all its fulness. Therefore 'your lips are' not an outpouring but 'a dripping honeycomb'. On the lips of the bride then is only sweetness and full sweetness and measured sweetness. Sweetness is indeed fully possessed, yet poured not fully but exactly as the capacity of the audience requires.

Do you also wish to hear the evidence from the very lips of the bride herself? 'How sweet are your words to my taste, sweeter than honey to my mouth.'*² Sweet indeed are the lips of the bride for the sayings of the Lord distill from her lips. This sweetness belongs to the sayings of the Lord. Indeed she does not speak on her own, but, as it were, delivers the messages of the Lord; therefore grace is poured upon her lips.* Hear now in part what kinds of honey the comb of the divine word distills and what amount God has allotted for each vessel into which honey is distilled.

The honeycomb of the divine word remits and permits, promises and prepares. It remits sins, permits infirmities, promises eternal blessings and prepares in advance some firstfruits of those blessings. It speaks wisdom among the perfect, wisdom indeed not of this world but God's wisdom hidden in

Ps 118:103

Ps 44:33

mystery,* and among those less spiritually wise it considers that it 'knows nothing but Christ Jesus and him crucified'.* His word encourages us toward perfection, it does not compel; still more, it consoles the fainthearted, bears up the weak and, if it corrects the restless, the correction itself has the taste of maternal sweetness.* His word has compassion on the sinner; it pardons the converted; it sets no measure or limit to its pardon beyond which it may not go, for we are commanded to forgive seventy times seven times a day one who confesses his sins that many times.*

3. See what a great store of sweetness is on the lips of the bride, who as often as you drift into evil,* if you be converted, so often drips honey into you for your good and is not exhausted by her role of pardoner. In Luke, like the angels of God she does not insult but instead exults over one repentant sinner.* Good then it is to lend a hearing to her lips. Indeed even the Lord bends his ear to her prayers and so challenges and invites your affection that he even betrays his own. Say what you have to say, O bride, for your Beloved listens eagerly whether you speak about him or whether you chat with him. But when the bride speaks with the Bridegroom himself, then she speaks with a sweeter song on her lips and she speaks with another tongue. Then the lips of her heart truly distill a honey of divine delight, or rather they do not so much distill as overflow, since at that hour her whole soul is changed into honeyed affections.

Blessed is the exchange, when from the heart of the bride some streams of honey flow into the Beloved and from him return in waves to the bride. Indeed to the source whence these rivers of honey emerge they are restored that they may continue to flow. Good are the honeycombs on the lips of Bridegroom and bride, rising from well-spring to well-spring and sharing with each other the dews of love's sweetness. He from on high drops down dews of grace;* she from below returns the dew of thanksgiving. Jesus himself has begotten the drops of this honeyed dew in the beloved soul. Wholly sweet are these drops of dew, the affections of divine love, when the bride is wholly dissolved into honeyed drops before the face of the One she loves, before the face of her God. Therefore her 'lips are like a dripping honeycomb', because passionately sweet is the ardor of a mind so affectionate; but the ardor is quickly cut short, because that rapture of the mind is sweet to excess and because all too soon it is interrupted.

4. 'Your lips are a dripping honeycomb.' I consider these lips entirely purified, for from them Jesus himself recalls that he draws honeyed sweetness. Isaiah's lips were purified by being touched with tongs and a coal from the altar.* 'The Lord put forth his hand,' says Jeremiah, 'and touched my mouth.'*³ One who is a bride desires not a coal, not a finger, but the touch of his lips. 'Let him kiss me,' she says, 'with the kiss of his mouth.'* Lips cry for lips. Nor indeed would sweetness be pressed from the bride's lips, if her lips did not receive the impress of her Beloved's lips. Yet in what else does he rejoice but in the sweetness of the kiss, which he steals from the bride's lips, when he says: 'Your lips are a dripping honeycomb'? Thanks to both, thanks to the kiss of charity and thanks to the utterance of truth, he says: 'Your lips are a dripping honeycomb; honey and milk are beneath your tongue.' Is 6:6-7

Jr 1:9

Sg 1:1

Milk beneath the tongue refers properly to the grace of speech. The lips are also used for a kiss but the tongue only for speech. Not only does sweetness ring upon the tongue but 'milk and honey are beneath your tongue'. Sweetness which is counterfeit rings only upon the tongue and is not tasted beneath the tongue. Slight is the sweetness, which is wholly on the lips and on the tongue and whose greater part is not beneath the tongue. Sweetness is not only on the bride's tongue or wholly on her tongue, but as he who knows bears witness: 'Milk and honey are beneath your tongue'. Therefore, she breaks out in a goodly word, a word both of honey and of milk, thanks to the majesty of his Godhead and thanks to the mystery of his Incarnation. Her tongue and her lips are like a silver channel through which streams of milk and honey bubble from the fountain of her heart. Each is sweet but their sweetness is different: milk is for babes, as Paul says,* while he also teaches a sweet and divine and, as it were, a honeyed wisdom for the perfect.*[4]

5. Some people have only honey beneath their tongues and no milk, others only milk and no honey. But beneath the bride's tongue are both alike, honey and milk. The bride does not pour but rather distills the honey; neither indeed does she pour at random and without restraint those sublime and hidden senses of heavenly secrets and the mysteries of the Godhead, nor does she give milk to drink without discretion. 'Honey and milk are beneath your tongue', says the Bridegroom. Indeed her message is neither devoid of inner sweetness nor equal to her own inner sweetness. A sweet message is on the tip of her tongue for 'beneath her tongue are honey and milk'.

Blessed is the tongue which distills like a honeycomb and is distended like breasts with milk for babes, which distills honey and flows with milk. All outcry, bitterness and blasphemy are banished far from these lips according to the persuasive warning of Paul.* Nor are 'fraud and oppression beneath her tongue' in the words of the Psalm,* but 'honey and milk are beneath your tongue' in the words of the Bridegroom. 'A dripping honeycomb are the lips of the harlot,' says the book of Proverbs 'and her throat is smoother than oil.' Yet neither milk nor honey is beneath her tongue, neither in her hidden way nor in her final day, 'but in the end she is bitter as wormwood, sharp as a two-edged sword'.*

Yet of the valiant woman the same book of Proverbs says: 'Strength and beauty are her clothing and she will laugh on the last day.'* Even now her mouth gives birth to that spiritual and really happy laughter and its sweetness, as it were, 'lies hidden beneath her tongue'. But the milk and honey which now lie under her tongue will bubble up into full happiness on the last day. Then joy will nowise be choked in silence beneath the tongue, but long suppressed it will burst out and fill her mouth with laughter,* the mouth of the woman, I repeat, 'whose clothing is strength and beauty'. Notice how improper it is for her to be discovered stripped of her clothing, who expects the promised joys to be given her.

Jb 8:21

6. Who knows whether these are not the same garments mentioned in the same verse of our Canticle: 'the fragrance of your garments is like the fragrance of incense'? 'I clothed my soul in fasting,' says the psalmist,* and again I shall 'humble my soul in fasting and my prayer will be folded back on my bosom'.* Fasting is a good garment and in its hidden bosom, as it were, prayer dwells. It is a garment with a fold like a bosom: 'My prayer shall be folded back on my bosom.' Here you have both, if you notice: in fasting, the cloak of strength; and in prayer, the fragrance of incense. 'My prayer shall be folded back on my bosom.'

Ps 68:11

Ps 34:13

Why then does he say 'on my bosom?' Does he wish us to understand perhaps the failure of lukewarm and interrupted prayer, vanishing in the very first upward motion? Is prayer then said to be 'folded back on its bosom', that is, to relapse into the very place whence it rose? But how is what perishes folded back and returned? That prayer seems rather to be 'folded back on its bosom' which quickly though not fully obtains what it seeks; at least in part it receives the reward of a humble and devout petition. Prayer, importunate and devout, has indeed much sweetness. While prayer rises in the sight of the Lord like incense,* it breathes in the sweet scent of its own fragrance. Is that not a good cloak, when the mist from such a cloud enfolds and invests the very soul of the suppliant? A good cloak it is, but as we have begun, so let us continue our interpretation of the garments in terms of outward actions.

Ps 140:2.
Lam 188, n. 118

7. Now good deeds both cover previous deformity, lest it be charged to our loss, and lend some beauty and charm that it may be counted as gain. Good garments then are the good deeds which

both grace the body and win grace for the soul. That they grace the body is obvious but not everyone's finery yields the fragrance of incense and displays a pattern of prayer. According to Scripture, when anyone's deeds, powerful for all to see,[5] smack of ostentation and vainglory,* not of insistent supplication, not of eagerness to please the Lord,* not of desires to win grace, how shall the scent of such a one's finery be compared to 'the fragrance of incense'?

But when a man does everything in order to please God with whom he enlisted* and to deserve his favor, certainly 'the fragrance of his garments is like the fragrance of incense'. Incense is wont to be offered and ought to be offered only to God; therefore 'the fragrance of his garments is like the fragrance of incense', since whatever he does whether openly or secretly is directed to obtaining divine propitiation. Oil in vessels seems to be the same as fragrance in garments, if it is the fragrance of incense. For what else but those spiritual joys and eternal delight does one ask of God, when one renounces and abhors all other delight?

'My soul thirsts for you,' says the Psalm, 'in how many ways does my flesh thirst for you!'* You see in these words how the very garment of the flesh plays the role of prayer, when the flesh is said to thirst for God. Does not the flesh which is afflicted by voluntary mortification strive to bend God to propitiation? The very sufferings of the flesh on God's account are supplications to him. Alms given in compassion to the poor implore him; why should the discreet curbing of one's own bodily pleasures not be as effective as prayer? The curbing of pleasure is an expression of one's yearnings and of a desire which sighs for a different delight. The result of fervent prayer returns and 'folds back upon the bosom of the heart'. Incense yields a sweet fragrance in the garment of outward abstinence.

Wholly good is the garment, when the soul is robed not so much in the flesh as in a chastening fast from pleasures of the flesh. Wholly good is the garment of virginal continence; like incense it wafts a sweet fragrance to him who is loved and to her who loves. Whatever is offered with love, she who makes the offering cannot fail to enjoy its delight. Indeed all this sweetness which is commended in her is also perceived by herself. From her it flows and in her it remains. On her lips is a honeycomb, beneath her tongue honey and in her garments the scent of incense. Closest to herself are these three gifts so pleasing to the senses, so sweet to enjoy. 'The words of my mouth will be pleasing,' says David, 'and the meditation of my heart ever in your sight.'* Here you have each of two gifts, and that nothing may be wanting to the fulness of grace, by the mention of 'garments' in the third place, is inserted the quality of good deeds. From the lips words drop; beneath the tongue flow honeyed meditations; the adornment of garments wafts the fragrance of incense. *Ps 18:15. Lam 186, n. 105.*

8. What do you think is absent from her glory, when in her these three gifts are equally pleasing: her lips, her spirit and her work? In this number all are included but reversed in their order. Indeed one must begin with works, not with words. The works and prayers of Cornelius the centurion were heard first. By faith their hearts were cleansed and then the Spirit descended upon him and his household and they spoke with tongues.* The apostles themselves after the Ascension of the Lord with one accord persevered in prayer;* then when the days assigned for the promise were complete they were filled with the Spirit,* and afterwards they set out and preached everywhere.* First was their prayer in profusion, then an infusion of the Spirit; so the grace they acquired, they poured in profusion for others. First in expectation and longing they were turned towards God; secondly God turned towards them; thirdly, once turned to God, they form and strengthen their brethren in his likeness.* *Ac 10:2, 46. Ac 1:14 Ac 2:4 Mk 16:20 Lk 22:32; Rm 8:29*

But whether you consider holiness of life in the apostles, God's visitation, or their ministry of the word,* all these take the place of garments, with all these they were covered and adorned. In them what *Ac 20:24* was left naked or shabby with its original stains, when they were brilliantly vested in the gay raiment of the word and of virtue? Splendid then was their raiment but not less was their influence. What perfume pours from their garments? What kind of fragrance have they? Is it not 'the fragrance of incense'? When they distribute their Lord's money to fellow servants, they do not allow a bit of it to remain with themselves even unobserved; they do not fraudently filch a coin for themselves. They shake their hands loose even from the tribute of praise,* attributing everything to the glory of God. Like the heavens they have been robed in beautiful light, but like the heavens they proclaim not their own glory but the glory of God.*

Paul himself by his words wove for you some delicate and incorruptible garments and according to your measure he fits you with a mantle of light and understanding, yet not in the plausible 'words of human wisdom but in the teaching of the Spirit'.* Therefore both the garments, with which he is covered himself and which he has woven for you, have the fragrance only of incense. An affected display of words seems to reek of the affectation of idle foppery and vanity. Those again who pursue not the charm of eloquence but hazardous and fallacious argumentation on recondite subjects, while they expend themselves unduly for an empty fame, sometimes weave in patches of blasphemy.⁶ So the fragrance of such a man's garments is not 'the fragrance of incense'. But not one of the bride's garments does the Bridegroom seem to exclude, since he commends without restriction: 'the fragrance of your garments is like the fragrance of incense'. Oh happy were I if even one or other garment upon me should yield the pure fragrance of incense, not spoiled by any foreign admixture! Indeed no one in my opinion has reached that stature where his whole wardrobe wafts the fragrance of incense, if he has not yet been found worthy to be elevated to the state of his brides by the Lord Jesus, the Bridegroom of brides.

NOTES ON SERMON THIRTY-FOUR

1.　G. writes for one individual, except in two early sentences of par. 1, and in the first half of par. 2. See à Lapide, 8:72.
2.　See de Lubac, *Exégèse Médiéval*, 1:615, n. 13.
3.　See Bernard, SC 1-8; Gilbert uses 'embrace' more often.
4.　See De Lubac, *Exégèse Médiéval*, 1:612.
5.　Reading *potentia* with mss Paris 9605, 8546, Bruges 49, Madrid 512, Troyes 917, rather than *patentia* of Mab. or *patientia* of Migne.
6.　See Horace's purple patch, *Ars Poetica*, lines 14-16.

SERMON 35
FRUITS OF THE FOUNTAIN
AND THE GARDEN

From the fountain in the garden the bride offers rich fruits. 1. The garden means interior delights and the enclosure means the discipline of standing watch. 2. Horticulture is useless without custody; Adam was a hapless guardian; we need custody for our spiritual garden. 3. This garden has a threefold praise; devotion inspires the heart and makes the seeds of virtue germinate. 4. A fountain constantly wells up and when sealed is not drained away; as the fountain is sealed with figures, the book is wrapped in riddles. 5. Like paradise is the conscience and behavior of the bride. 6. The pomegranate shows the kinship of modesty and patience. 7. Religious congregations are likened to pomegranates.

A GARDEN ENCLOSED ARE YOU, SISTER, MY BRIDE, A GARDEN ENCLOSED, A FOUNTAIN SEALED. YOUR SPRAYS ARE A PARADISE OF POMEGRANATES, WITH THE CHOICEST OF FRUITS, . . . *[1] *Sg 4:12-13*

Agarden are you, sister, my bride, a garden enclosed, a fountain sealed.' From his words, weigh first the affection of this panegyrist. He seems delighted, since he is not content with one eulogy. How great his affection would have been, if without repetition he had spoken a simple eulogy of the lady he addresses! Now however he adopts recherché terms of courtesy and in tribute doubles his compliments. Why should he not? Will he not doubly rejoice in the precious endowments of the one he chose for the grace of matrimony? Only one who was worthy could be chosen for the privileges of such sweet intimacy, nor once chosen could she be loved lukewarmly. Is it not right that she also should strive to please him in such privileges, since he has given her such praise? He praises her, he prepares her to match his praise, he plants her for himself as a paradise of pleasure. He who personally prepares her to match his praise, personally compares her to a paradise of delights.

'Behold,' said Isaac, 'the fragrance of my son is like the fragrance of a bountiful field, which the Lord has blessed.'* Yet his bride is compared not to a field but to a garden, for there the planting of flowers seems spiritual and the cultivation of spices more bountiful. Into this garden, good Jesus, you readily descend to the beds of spices, to recline in this garden, to be its gardener and its guardian. 'A garden enclosed,' he says, 'sister, my bride, a garden enclosed.' Take the garden, brethren, to mean interior delights and the enclosure the discipline of standing watch. Whom will you liken to a garden, but one whose soul is as quickened with the scent of spiritual affections as a garden with perfumed flowers? What a pleasant sanctuary,[2] what a sweet retreat in the bride's breast, a breast so luxuriant with flowers that it is compared to a garden!

There no 'root of bitterness springing up',* chokes the delights of this garden. 'Every plant which my heavenly Father has not planted'* will not be found in it. In Scripture, he himself planted this pleasure garden, that he alone might cultivate and guard it.* He cultivates it in two ways, by planting and by weeding. He plants it that every seed may be true to him, but he weeds it 'that it may bear more fruit'.* It is planted that the seed may be true and it is weeded that it may not be half empty. What is the point of planting for truth, if failure to weed does not provide abundance? The diligent cultivation of

Gn 27:27.
Lam 19, n. 83.

Heb 12:15

Mt 15:13

Gn 2:8, 15

Jr 2:21; Jn 15:2

discipline yields nothing without watch and ward. He lacks neither, who is likened to a garden and to a 'garden enclosed'.

2. 'A garden enclosed are you, sister, my bride.' Over the garden in which he was placed, Adam kept a poor watch against the slithering entry of the wily serpent. Pleasant indeed was that paradise of material trees, but I envisage a much fairer paradise planted in Adam's spirit. The serpent would have invaded that material garden harmlessly, if it had not squirmed into the garden of the spirit. The snake was welcomed and at once Adam felt deeply its venom, for 'a snake will bite someone who breaches a wall'.* A wall is a good protection, for a wall separates and keeps unharmed what is cultivated from what is not. Surround your garden then with this wall, lest, if the wall be removed and its cement crumbled, you become exposed to plunder and trampling. *Qo 10:8*

Adam's garden was not closed to his enemy but thereafter how heavily it was barred to Adam the outcast and exile! With no ease does Adam reenter the garden, from which with careless ease he fell.* In the sweat of his brow does he eat bread, who in paradise at will plucked fruit from the tree of life.* Here he eats his bread, there the fruits of life. In paradise 'the Lord . . . brought forth every tree fair to look upon and delicious to eat'.* Adam the outcast digs in the earth; not the Lord but the earth itself yields thorns and thistles for its cultivator. Paradise yields its fruit without labor but the earth fails to yield despite the laborer. It is a pitiful change but 'you destroy', O Lord, and justly, every 'unfaithful fornicator'.* Rightly is he destroyed, who by fornication destroys such intimate bonds and no longer deserves to hear such terms of endearment as the words 'sister', 'bride', 'garden' and 'garden enclosed', which admits none but the Beloved. *Heb 6:6* *Gn 3:2* *Gn 2:9* *Ps 72:27*

Let the door of your paradise be ever closed but opened only to your Prince. Let its panels not be 'broken down with hammer and hatchet'.* There let one entrance be built and this entrusted to the Cherubim. Let nothing be admitted which has not *Ps 73:6* first been tested by their 'flaming sword', nothing which the word of God may reject, which charity may not approve, which may not approach the perfection and 'fulness of the law'.* So the Cherubim are fulness of knowledge and charity is the fulness of the law; in charity are included all the commandments.* Let charity be for you a flaming guard, to consume at once without delay anything unworthy which attempts to break in. Is enclosure not aptly attributed to love, which always controls the feelings of the bride and encloses them in Love Itself, ever turning her inwards where her delights may be to dwell with the Son of God?*

A good wall is love but this wall has a rampart in front of it. Love is like a wall and its rampart is the strictness of the Rule. The wall encloses holy thoughts and sweet affections; the rampart repulses and shuts out occasions of sin. The rampart of the Rule affords the opportunity of leisure for the attentions of love; the wall of love enjoys them.³ The inner wall is pleasing; the outer rampart is necessary. The wall encloses you amid heavenly delights; the rampart excludes worldly pleasures. If it is your desire to offer your heart to Christ as a garden of delights, do not take it ill if you are enclosed by this rampart. Anyone who complains of a bulwark wishes to lose the delights he possesses, if indeed he does possess them. One who knows not how to be enclosed, knows not how to be a garden.

3. 'A garden enclosed, a fountain sealed. Your sprays are a paradise of pomegranates, with the choicest of fruits.' The Bridegroom completes the praises of this garden in three points: it is enclosed and watered and perfumed. Enclosure confers freedom from care; irrigation adds fruitfulness; perfume concerns both the products of the garden and their charm. Does this garden not seem charming to us, so replete, so rich and so useful? Not only is the garden useful, but it also abounds in perfumed delights. Who among us would dare to attribute these praises to himself? Who would assume that these compliments are for

himself? As we appreciate the irrigation and germination of spices, so would that we did not depreciate the enclosure and the seal. Indeed only a garden enclosed and irrigated by the streams of a sealed fountain produces these sprays of spices. Let your fountain then be sealed, that it may not be totally dried up by reckless outpouring; let it be sealed, that it may satisfy your need for irrigation.

'Distribute your streams through your squares; keep them to yourself, that strangers may not be your partners.'* In the squares, I say, but in your own squares, distribute your waters, that the spices of the virtues may grow for you as if by the water in the squares.* How shall he not be a fountain sealed, who flows from that fountain of life which 'God the Father sealed'?* Whoever will drink of this water which I give, says the Lord, 'it will become in him a spring of water welling up to eternal life'.* In this fountain which the Beloved describes as 'sealed', understand a teaching that is sealed and spiritual and personal and withdrawn from the world—yes, either a teaching or certainly a devotion, sealed with the privilege of sweetness and, as it were, especially one's own, flowing abundantly and continuously. This is the fountain which creates all the joyful fruits of the virtues. This is the stimulant for valiant deeds, like marrow for their bones.* For this joy, this personal and peerless devotion to God, refreshes the countenance of the heart.* It is like a sealed fountain of one's own set apart for this service:* to water the heart of the bride, who is like a garden meant for the delights of the Bridegroom. *Pr 5:16* *Rv 22:2* *Jn 6:27* *Jn 4:13-14* *Pr 3:8* *Pr 15:13* *Rm 1:1*

Let the fountain then be sealed, lest it become in the words of Proverbs 'your spring muddied by the foot, a polluted fountain'.* Otherwise your Beloved knows not how to drink from a pure fountain. 'The light of your countenance, O Lord,' says the psalmist, 'has been sealed upon us; you have given joy to my heart.'* Apply the rejoicing to irrigation. In Psalms, the garden germinating shall rejoice in the rivulets from the fountain.* Do you not recall how in Genesis a fountain began to rise and to water the *Pr 25:6* *Ps 4:7* *Ps 64:11* the whole surface of the earth?* The earth still gave only its fruits; it was not yet acquainted with thorns and thistles. Who will give this water to my little garden and this fountain sealed to my flower beds? Who will grant that the whole surface of my little garden may be watered with rivulets of delight and of light, that nothing in it may either be barren or saddened by lack of devotion? Cheerless activity, deprived of the irrigation of spiritual joy, seems close to barrenness. In the words of Scripture, even if something sprouts, it grows 'like a root from parched land'.* Like a root it is, not like flowers, not like fruit; like a root, with little or nothing more than a root.

4. The fountain was introduced to encourage your belief that flourishing plants spring up in a watered garden. There exists indeed a garden, whose waters come by chance and, as it were, are imported from without, not perennial, not part of the garden. Good is the garden, however, when its fountain rises from within. A fountain sealed and belonging to the garden, as the Bridegroom says, is 'a fountain' and a 'fountain sealed', that is, constantly welling up from within and unable to be polluted. 'A fountain' because it flows in abundance; 'sealed' because nowhere is it drained away. Or perhaps hers is called 'a sealed fountain' because, while others have other fountains, for his sister and bride there exists a special fountain of her own, one sealed by some particular privilege.

Entirely good is the fountain of wisdom,* but it still flows to us beneath a seal; its taste is delicious but it is not yet sparklingly clear for us. It is sealed and enclosed in figures. In the Apocalypse, a book sealed with seven seals is displayed in the hand of 'one seated upon a throne'.* The meaning of each, both of the fountain and of the book, points to the understanding of wisdom; but each is sealed with figures and wrapped in riddles. Each is sealed but through each wisdom is channelled to us through disclosures and hidden from us in the same disclosures. As in the Apocalypse you read of the openings of the sealed book, so here also you read of the sprays of the sealed fountain.⁴ 'Your sprays are a paradise of pomegranates with the choicest of fruits.' This fountain is indeed sealed but not dried up, since its sprays are so full of grace. Sealed is the fountain of wisdom but by its sprays you shall know it.

'There shall be a fountain opened for the House of David,' says Zechariah, 'to cleanse them from sin and from uncleanness.'* That fountain is open but this is sealed; that washes away but this washes in. That fountain cleanses but this irrigates. That purifies from sins but this produces delights. That fountain is shared by many but this is reserved for the bride. In Zechariah's fountain is remission of sins, in the bride's the emission of sprays. In a psalm for the octachord, see how first the psalmist floods his bed with tears, then drenches his couch with weeping,⁵ for it is not enough to be scoured from filth unless fruitfulness follows after.

Zc 13:1

5. 'Your sprays are a paradise of pomegranates.' *Yes, good Jesus, this is so. These sprays are your inspiration, inspirations channelled through good angels. The fountain could not spray such delights, unless you from within channelled the delights of living water.* 'The light of your countenance, O Lord, has been sealed upon us; you have given joy to my heart.'* That has been sealed upon us which has been impressed upon us from on high. When the image of the divine light from on high is impressed upon anyone, abundance of spiritual joy is expressed deep within the heart. Therefore the glorious sprays of the king's daughter are from deep within. 'Your sprays are a paradise.'* Not slender are the stores of delights within, when from them sprouts a whole paradise.

Ps 4:7

Sg 4:13

You have both, a paradise enclosed and a paradise produced. The former exists in affections of purity; the latter in acts of piety. Pure affection is within and pious action proceeds from it and tests it. Each is delightful: both the conscience and the behavior of the bride. For she both proposes all things usefully and disposes them well.* Accordingly you may see,

Ws 8:1; 1 Tm 4:6

as it were, a paradise in her outward demeanor and activity; her integrity makes her pleasing in each single action, her order when her actions are compared and her charm when her actions are summed up. She does everything with moderation and calm, that the serenity of virginal modesty in her may not be ruffled. In the Canticle, the Bridegroom, intending to list the blessings of this paradise, begins with modesty, proposing pomegranates as its symbol, thanks to their likeness in color. 'Your sprays are a paradise of pomegranates.'

6. Pomegranates can also be understood as the patience of the martyrs, because they have been stained red by their own blood. Yes, patience is a good companion to modesty; they are combined by James in the praise of wisdom: 'The wisdom from above is first pure, then peaceful.'* Modesty controls itself decorously and according to its rank, while patience bears with equanimity a lack of restraint in others. Modesty sets the style for its own actions; patience is a shield against the attacks of others. The one is style, the other strength. Therefore in Proverbs it is said: 'Strength and beauty are her clothing.'* 'It is first pure,' said James, 'then peaceful', and after a few words he adds, full of good works.* Good indeed it is to suffer persecution but for the fruits of justice.* Hence her sprays are pomegranates but with the choicest of fruits. Good indeed is modesty provided it be not idle, not affected, not hypocritical, but bearing fruit in patience. Modesty disposes sweetly, patience protects valiantly. One is decorous, the other longsuffering. Wherefore to both are linked 'the choicest of fruits' as the consummation and end of their activities.

7. We should have passed on now to treat of the aromatic trees, the more delicate species, the sprays of henna and nard, if the pomegranates were not still drawing us by their fragrance and delaying our sermon from hastening to other topics. The parable of the pomegranates regards ourselves, for by rule we live together in communities and are united in one Order like seeds beneath one rind. Yes, may we

imitate these seeds, resembling them not only by unanimity in union of heart but also by the embrace, as it were, of our Order. Practically indistinguishable in appearance, the seeds of the pomegranate cling together; they are distinguishable rather by numerical individuation than by appearance. Let us also learn to differ from one another in number, not in spirit. Seeds neither quarrel with one another, not grumble about the rind, nor try to break through it. They patiently permit themselves, as it were, to be shut up in its core, that somehow they may seem to say: 'Behold, how good and pleasant it is, when brethren dwell in unity'!*[6] In this Order of ours, brothers, as if in the rind of a pomegranate, does not the color of Christ's passion glow red by our imitation? Yes, like the seeds of this fruit are they who consider it second nature to be united under the rind of regular discipline and regard themselves not as constrained but as protected.[7] Let there be no love of property, no love of private ownership and then you appear as a seed of this fruit. Allured by our example, let others learn 'how good and how pleasant it is to dwell' in close communion and beneath the defence of a rind. Let charity unite and the rind defend. However many communities of an Order you see, regard all as so many pomegranates which have issued from the fountain of baptism. Yes, as we read, 'the believers had one heart and one soul'.* From believers as from the seeds of so many congregations living in an orderly way and in unity of spirit, pomegranates have developed. Those first communities of believers were not yet bound by the institute of any Order but by the impulse of love. To dwell in unity they considered not only useful, not only good but also pleasant, like the ointment 'which flowed down on the beard, the beard of Aaron, to the hem of his robe',* from the Head himself, Christ Jesus, who lives and reigns for ever and ever. Amen.

Ps 132:1

Ac 4:32

Ps 132:1-2.
Lam 15-16,
nn. 55, 57,
61, 62, 19;
n. 80.

NOTES ON SERMON THIRTY-FIVE

1. G. addresses one individual, except in the first two-thirds of par. 1, and in par. 7, where also *te exhibes* occurs. Jean Leclercq has summarized and set in their context Gilbert's three sermons, 35-37, in his article 'The Monastic Tradition of Culture and Studies', *American Benedictine Review*, 11 (1960) 99-131, esp. pp. 116-117. See also Emile Bertaud, 'Hortus, hortulus, Jardin Spirituel', in DSp 7 (1969) 766-784, and for later influence: Stanley Stewart, *The Enclosed Garden: tradition and image in seventeenth-century poetry* (Madison: U. of Wisconsin Press, 1966). Other sermons of Gilbert speak of the garden of wisdom, of the bride, of the Bridegroom, of delights and of heaven; see index.
2. Reading *penetrale* with mss Paris 9605 (apparently), 8546, Madrid 512, Mab. for *penetral* of ms Bruges 49, Troyes 419, or *penetrat* of Migne.
3. Leclercq, 'Otia Monastica,' 92:46.
4. Wisdom is channelled to us both through the fountain and the book; but both, in disclosing Wisdom, leave Wisdom enclosed and hidden. 'Sprays' of the translation is ambiguous; it includes both the sprays of water from the fountain and the sprays or plants which spring up from irrigation. See à Lapide, 8:76.
5. Ps 6:7. *Pro octava* appears in the Vulg. title of Psalms 6 and 11, and in 1 Ch 15:21, *in citharis pro octava canebant epinicion*. Three cantors 'were to clash the cymbals of bronze', eight players 'were to play the keyed harp', and six others 'giving the beat, were to play the *octave lyre*', 1 Ch 15:20-21 in the translation of The Jerusalem Bible. Thanks to some help from the monks of *Notre Dame des Prairies*, I can say: a) that Psalm 6 *pro octava*, the first of the penitential psalms, was neither appropriate for nor used for a feast or its octaves; b) that Hebrew music did not observe our diatonic scale; c) that commentators suggest either an eight-stringed instrument, *pro octava*, or d) according to the shemînîth, a lower pitch for harps, in contrast with the alamoth or higher pitch for psalteries.
6. See à Lapide, 8:79.
7. Leclercq, 'Disciplina', in DSp 3 (1957) 1291-1302.

SERMON 36
THE SPICES OF ALL THE VIRTUES

The bride produces spices of all the virtues. 1. In Scripture, the number seven means perfection or spirituality. 2. The meaning of the mystical trees; labor is sweetened by love or joy. 3. Action and contemplation blend into the fruits of the Spirit. 4. The meaning of henna, nard, and saffron. 5. The Bridegroom adapts his teaching to the capacity of his audience. 6. Some trees of our time lack faith and virtue. 7. The four cardinal virtues: fortitude in cedar, faith which informs prudence in Lebanon, temperance, self-control and justice in myrrh, and purity in aloes.

YOUR SPRAYS ARE A PARADISE OF POMEGRANATES, WITH THE CHOICEST OF FRUITS, HENNA WITH NARD, NARD AND SAFFRON, CALAMUS AND CINNAMON, WITH ALL TREES OF FRANKINCENSE, MYRRH AND ALOES, WITH ALL CHIEF SPICES[1]*   *Sg 4:13*

We must begin with henna, for there we ended. Here are listed seven aromatic trees which are said to sprout from the sealed fountain. Indeed these words seem to be the words of a sealed book.* Yes, the words are sealed and locked. Why do you set before us, good Jesus, the praises of your bride, if you yourself do not disclose what meaning they lock inside?[2] You hold the key of this garden enclosed; you have

See S 35:4

sealed it. Please unseal it! Please unfasten it! Please unfasten, I pray, these seven seals! No one knows what are those intimacies of the bride, those secrets of yours with which her interior is filled. No one knows but you and someone to whom you choose to reveal them.* Would that we too might be the ones who could contemplate with face unveiled the glory of the bride which is from within.* Great is her glory in the mystery both of this number and of these names.

Here, as far as by the Lord's gift we can make out, the hidden meaning of the number seven indicates either the spirituality or the universality of graces. Indeed it is a frequent practice of sacred Scripture to use the number seven to designate gifts which are perfect and come from above. There are 'varieties of gifts' and 'varieties of ministries' and 'varieties of services', but 'the same Spirit who apportions to each one as he wills'.* He allots some gifts to some and other gifts to others, but in the bride he collects, as it were, and assembles all together. They are not allotted to her one by one, as if they were divided in her. To others he both apportions and grants; to her he does not so much apportion as grant the whole; unless you understand him to apportion, in as much as he gives her[3] what is choice and privileged, either more graces of the same genus or more in another species. He might have listed other aromatic trees but seven are enough for that meaning we mentioned, either spirituality or universality.

2. Now let us discuss the names and natures of these trees. It seems pleasant to linger beneath their shade and their fruit will be sweet to our palate. Their shadow I take to be the symbol, their fruit the reality. How will the fruit of their interpretation not be sweet, when their names sound as pleasant as the rustling of leaves? And you know what a joyful feeling the repetition of such musical words gives to your ear. These words could have been enough to arouse your aesthetic sense. Indeed their simplicity is enough for this sense, yet not enough for the understanding. We must humor the understanding, which longs to

Mt 11:27

2 Co 3:18;
Ps 44:14

1 Co 12:4-11

feed on the truth in our sensations. The refrain of these musical words rings pleasantly in the ear: 'Henna with nard, nard and saffron, calamus and cinnamon, myrrh and aloes.' Perish the thought that their meaning is not much more pleasing!

Great are our bodily delights in the trees listed here, but how much greater are the spiritual delights which are symbolized by them! 'Your sprays,' says the Bridegroom, 'are a paradise of pomegranates'; they are also 'henna with nard'. Good indeed is this sequence: after the labors of patience, after the shyness of modesty, to progress to ointments and royal ointments. Yes, from the seed of henna also a royal ointment is wont to be compounded. Now as in pomegranates we understood the unity of spirit under a Rule, so in these words and in royal ointments interpret some surpassing sublimity. 'He who humbles himself,' says the Lord, 'shall be exalted.'* In patience and unity of spirit what is meant but humility? Humility neither rages against the insolent nor overreaches its comrades. In pomegranates then is humility, in henna sublimity; in the former toil, in the latter delights.

Lk 14:11.
Lam 15, n. 56.

The seed of henna, they say, is wont to be boiled in oil, that ointment may be pressed from it.[4] Others sow seeds in tears, but the bride in oil.[5] Our seeds are our good deeds. If these show cheerfulness they are, as it were, boiled in oil. To be dipped in oil is not sufficient; they must be cooked and compounded in oil and, as it were, changed into the oil itself. What is boiled in hot oil is steeped in the nature of oil itself. The seed of henna and the oil are cooked and compounded into an ointment of one consistency. Wonderful indeed is the compound of labor and laughter, so much more wonderful because in labor not the labor but the laughter alone is experienced. Indeed when work is boiled in the oil of exultation work passes into the essence of the oil. Work itself, so to speak, forgets it is work, while it is wholly steeped in the unction of love. But even interior exultation itself is strengthened and thrives on work; thus indeed the seed contributes to the oil and the oil to the seed, when the bride sets out to work with exultation and thanks to her work, exults the more.

3. This ointment is for royalty. Jesus himself is gladly anointed with it 'for God loves a cheerful giver'.* Although 'God the Father anointed him with spirit and power',* although he was 'anointed with the oil of gladness more than his fellows',* he wishes to be anointed by his fellows and longs for the ointment of our devotion. Who will give me such a store of oil, that in this oil all the fruits of my works can be boiled and my heart wholly dissolved? John the Evangelist, an example of contemplative life and a symbol of the bride, was lowered into a cauldron full of boiling oil.[6] Who will give me such abundance of oil and of boiling oil that I may be wholly immersed and compounded? Who will give me such abundance of oil and henna seed as may suffice for the compounding of ointment? This boiling in oil does not accept every seed, does not welcome every fruit. Scripturally, not every work can be mingled with the gladness of contemplation.* Works involving outward solicitude and the practice of contemplation cannot be compounded together or jell into one kind of ointment.

What fruits then does this compounding accept? Those to be sure which the apostle lists: The fruits of the Spirit are joy, peace, patience, longanimity, faith, meekness, modesty, self-control, chastity.* These fruits blend with the oil of contemplation and, as it were, join together into a natural unity. But especially suited to this compounding is that seed of which the Lord speaks: 'The seed is the Word of God.'* In Scripture also the seed of henna has some resemblance to manna, which we take as a symbol of the Word of God. For each of the two, manna and henna seed, is white and like coriander seed.*

The law of the Lord is spotless.* His law does not want to be diluted with the water of worldly wisdom nor to be strengthened by worldly maxims but by the oil of the Spirit, that its spiritual meaning and the unction of the Spirit may be pressed from his law. Meditation on the law and the joy of contemplation are most readily blended, when zeal for the word and the oil of grace are joined together in contemplation, and provided the one is boiled in the other, from the process is readily expressed that understanding and unction of the Spirit which 'teaches about all things'.* Notice also that our text does not say simply 'henna' but 'henna with nard'. The Lord admits that he was anointed with nard in preparation for his burial.* What else then do you understand in 'nard' but peace of mind? This nard then is joined with henna, because all practice of contemplation needs peace of mind.

1 Jo 2:27

Mt 26:12. See à Lapide, 8:80.

4. 'Henna with nard, nard and saffron', says the Bridegroom. A good association, for saffron, a flower of a golden color, is related to the golden hue of wisdom. Therefore by henna is meant investigation, by nard vacation and by saffron the vision of wisdom.[7] Nard is rightly placed in the center as a prerequisite for both investigation and vision. For without mental leisure, truth can neither be investigated nor, if it be found, can it be envisioned. Translate henna then as study, nard as leisure and saffron as the fruit of both. In future do not say, O bride, do not say that 'I am swarthy'; call yourself colorless no longer.* For now, on the evidence of the Bridegroom himself, you are resplendent with the color of saffron, because you are radiant in saffron. Rightly is she resplendent with the hue of saffron, for silliness does not make her swarthy, nor does tedium or faintheartedness dye her the color of death, but the golden hue of wisdom and the radiant glow of charity reflects her merriment.

Sg 1:5. See à Lapide, 8:80.

5. Should we wish to refer these plants to the person of Christ, clearly an apt meaning results. Who has been more steeped in the boiling oil of grace? He is recognized in manna; he assumes the appearance of henna seed; pressed on the Cross of his Passion he poured out the mysteries of salvation and the ointments of grace. He suffers in henna, is buried in nard, and in saffron he rises again from the heart of the earth. He is like a fresh and radiant bloom when through his Resurrection his flesh blossomed anew.

And perhaps he ascends into heaven as the calamus. This tree grows high indeed. His bride shares his suffering, as it were, in henna, is buried with him in nard, and rises with him in saffron. What follows but that she should ascend with him in calamus? For if she has risen with the Bridegroom, she must 'seek the things which are above', develop her 'taste for things above', where her Bridegroom is 'enthroned at the right hand of God'.*

'Calamus and cinnamon.' Calamus rises high; cinnamon hardly lifts its head from the ground. As the calamus she looks aloft, but as cinnamon she refrains from lofty thoughts.*[8] The calamus mounts high, the cinnamon bends low. The bride is the calamus when she is carried off to God; she is the cinnamon when she bends down to us. Although she bends down to us, all she brings forth is spiritual. Indeed when cinnamon is broken, it emits a visible incense. But when is it broken, if not when it is opened, when it is exposed? So indeed when Jesus took bread, he broke and shared it.* As a teacher accommodating himself, as it were, he breaks himself when he begins to open himself, to disembowel himself of the mysteries from on high which lie hidden within him, to disgorge from his memory his store of sweetness.* This is why as broken cinnamon he is said to emit a visible incense. Why an incense and why visible? An incense because what he utters is spiritual; visible because he teaches openly.*

Now the man who slips from the sublime to the ridiculous and to empty tales does not bend down but falls on his face. He does indeed speak in a broken voice but he does not emit a sweet incense. Like calamus sprouting in water, he rises high amid prayerful tears. Beautiful is your ascent, but take care that your descent be like cinnamon. When some reasonable cause recalls and restrains you from that ascent and transport, be like cinnamon. Let your chats and your ordinary behavior have the incense of grace. And if sometimes you are diverted from your will and resolve, let your will be bent and, as it were, broken to the will of an elder; let no murmur be heard, no complaint. Be cinnamon; emit the incense of grace and not an insulting remark. The reason why broken cinnamon emits a visible incense is that the virtue of humility makes progress and is tested in the weakness of being distressed and, as it were, of being broken. This is called both incense and visible: incense because tranquillity is preserved in your heart; visible because tranquillity reflects on your countenance.

6. To these plants the Bridegroom adds all the trees of Lebanon. Notice too that he lists none but the trees of Lebanon and omits none which belong to Lebanon: 'With all the trees of Lebanon,' he says. Trees of Lebanon are free from rot because they are of cedar and are pure because they are of Lebanon. Only the trees of the Church possess 'the mystery of faith in a pure conscience'* and, as it were, immunity from rot thanks to self-control; only the trees of Lebanon possess both purity and permanence. A good tree is obviously a man of the Church in whom strength of discipline and beauty of faith merge and meet. Strength and beauty are his clothing.*

1 Tm 3:9

Pr 31:25

In our day some trees have sprung up which the heavenly Father did not plant, trees not planted in our Lebanon. They make a display of strength in activity, of indifference to insults, of endurance in scarcity. They appear to be of cedar but not the cedar of Lebanon, because their mind and conscience are unclean. Indeed 'to unbelievers nothing is clean'.* The bravery flaunted with a flourish in their behavior becomes rotten in their profession of faith. What glitters, as it were, in their behavior, in their faith offends the nostrils. In their work, of course, piety is apparent; in their questioning, unbelief is patent. Their strength is the strength of a stone and their flesh is of bronze.* To be sure they are true to their father, of whom the Lord speaks in Job: 'His heart is as a stone, unyielding as a blacksmith's anvil.'*

Tt 1:15

Jb 6:12

Jb 41:15

Perversely brave are they, not for the faith but against the faith. Indeed the Almighty has not softened their hearts, has not softened or cleansed or made them white by faith; therefore they are not trees of Lebanon. 'Whatever does not proceed from faith is sin';* how much more sinful then is what attacks the faith! They are not trees of Lebanon whom purity of faith does not water. Barren are virtues not made fertile through faith, and even faith itself without virtues is dead.* No rot of incontinence defiles the purity of faith. In trees of the Church both meet: the beauty of faith and the strength of good deeds. Such a cedar is planted in our Lebanon. Here and not elsewhere exists the purity of faith and, as it were, a durable and incorrupt perseverance in virtue.

7. Yes, here 'myrrh and aloes with all chief spices' flourish. These spices are known to preserve from corruption even what of itself is liable to corruption. After the cedars of Lebanon why should the garden grow these spices, if they are indistinguishable from cedar? Although cedars and spices seem similar, they have their differences. The trees of Lebanon in themselves possess freedom from corruption, while myrrh and aloes impart incorruptibility to what is corruptible. Cedars are immune from rot, spices communicate such immunity. He is a good tree then and rightly planted in the Lord's paradise, on his noble mountain, on Mount Lebanon, who restrains himself from disintegrating through lawlessness and by the myrrh of his message makes others immune to such disintegration, for his body is like cedar and from his lips myrrh is distilled.

'Myrrh and aloes with all chief spices.' In our interpretation, we can refer these spices to the four cardinal virtues, if in cedar we understand fortitude, in Lebanon faith which fashions prudence itself, in myrrh temperance, self-control and justice, and in aloes purity, for the gum of this tree is said to be a purgative. By myrrh then outward actions are restrained; by aloes inward actions are not feigned hypocritically. In these now you have expressed the four cardinal virtues: first constancy, lest you 'believe for a while and in the time of temptation fall away';* then prudence, that your service may be

Sermon Thirty-Six

reasonable;* thus the myrrh of bodily mortification will follow, when you have zeal according to knowledge; in the fourth place aloes, when the heart itself is offered and burnt in sacrifice, so that together there may be in myrrh mortification of the flesh* and in aloes cleansing of the conscience from dead works to serve the living God,* lest we serve to please the eye or to give satisfaction to men instead of to God.* Is not the bride truly blessed, to whom so many terms of endearment are spoken? Much has been entrusted to her, for she manifests so many gifts pleasing to her Beloved.[9] For in all these he glories and he compliments his bride on her gifts, Jesus Christ who lives and reigns for ever and ever. Amen.

Rm 12:1

2 Co 4:10

Heb 9:14

Col 3:22

NOTES ON SERMON THIRTY-SIX

1. G. addresses one individual, except in the first sentences of par. 2, scitis.
2. Reading *veritatis* with mss Paris 9605, 8546, Bruges 49, Madrid 512, Troyes 419, rather than *virtutis* preferred by Mab. and Migne.
3. Reading *illi* with mss and Migne for *ilii* of Mab.
4. Reading *exprimatur* with mss Paris 9605, 8546, Bruges 49, Madrid 512, Troyes 419, for *exprimitur* of Mab.
5. Reading a period after *oleo* with mss and Mab. but omitted by Migne.
6. Jerome, *Adversus Jovinianum*, 1:26, who quotes Tertullian, *De praescriptione*, 36.
7. Leclercq, 'Otia Monastica,' 120:32.
8. See à Lapide, 8:81; Jean Leclercq, 'Caelestis Fistula,' in *Verbum et Signum*, Erster Band, Beiträge zur mediävistischen Bedeutungsforschung (Wilhelm Fink Verlag, Munich, 1975) 59-68.
9. Reading *dilecto* with mss and Mab, for *dilectio* of Migne.

SERMON 37
A WELL AND A FOUNTAIN,
WISDOM AND LOVE

The lover is a well and a fountain, wise and loving. 1. The fountain in the garden is unfailingly fruitful. 2. Irrigating the flower beds of the virtues. 3. The gardens growing in monastic houses distinguish monastic from secular perfection. 4. How wells and fountains differ. 5. How acquired and infused wisdom differ; dispositions needed for wisdom. 6. There are wells of quarrel and accusation, heretical and schismatic. 7. Worldly pleasures are deceptive and fleeting; knowledge of mysteries here is obscure, there is clear. 8. The violence of love; faith and Christ compared to Lebanon. 9. The faithful were once unconquerable against persecution; caution against soft and lukewarm monks.

A FOUNTAIN OF GARDENS, A WELL OF LIVING WATERS, WHICH FLOW IN A TORRENT FROM LEBANON*[1]   *Sg 4:15*

A fountain of gardens, a well of living waters, which flow in a torrent from Lebanon.' At the beginning of this passage the bride was called a fountain and now at the end her Beloved greets her with the title of fountain. She begins in fruitfulness and her fruitfulness grows with her years;* the ending corresponds with the begin-   *Ps 91:15* ning. Many are the sprays of this fountain but the bride is not exhausted by these sprays. She does not run dry with the passing of time; she is not drained by this overflow. At the beginning of this passage she is called a 'fountain sealed',* and here is a hint that the fountain did not run dry. There is taught the quality of the sprays, here how unfailing they are. Copious streams of graces flow from this fountain and yet the fountain always goes on.² This fountain does not withdraw from its origin and so both there and here is called a fountain.

But now notice where its waters flow. Where but in gardens? Indeed this is a fountain of gardens and it flows gently because it does not desert the gardens; it is not meant to cleanse but to irrigate; its whole purpose is not to scour filth but to increase fruitfulness. To use a fountain for scouring is good but to use it to increase fertility is better. One washes out stains, the other leaves deposits of graces as if in a delta; one makes plants clean, the other makes them luxuriant. One is open for the scouring of the sinner and of the menstruant woman,* the other is sealed for the delights the other is sealed for the delights of the bride. blemish in you.'* Therefore she is called a fountain only of gardens, a fountain of delights.

2. From our text, as the measure of heavenly delights is varied and multiple, so the number of gardens seems to be multiplied. One is all red with the rose, another all white with the lily, and a third all purple with violets. There are as many gardens as there are flower beds of virtues. Where one lonely flower blooms, who will claim that a garden is there? So neither one plant of chastity nor one of justice can satisfy the fulness of a garden. Solomon, who was called delicate and gentle,* laid out for himself gardens and orchards and planted them with trees of every kind. He does not say, 'I planted them with a tree' but 'with trees', not 'of one kind' but 'of every kind'. 'I constructed for myself,' he says, 'pools of water to irrigate the forest of budding trees.'* He was indeed rich in delights, for he possessed not a scattering of trees, few enough to be numbered and recorded, but a whole forest, 'a forest of budding trees'. In the garden of wisdom, of course, nothing is

barren, no plant is without buds.

Thus the bride too has many gardens and she is richly planted with saplings of virtue of every kind. In a later chapter also the Bridegroom compliments the bride in the words: 'Since you dwell in my gardens my friends harken to you; make me hear your voice.'* And with every right! For what is it but pleasant to harken to her who dwells in gardens and speaks from gardens? Her voice is not heard in the streets or outside the garden; therefore he is a friend who dwells with her in gardens. He is not so much in gardens as he is the garden himself. She is a garden and he is a fountain watering her gardens with the streams of his teaching. Happy is the bride whose only business is to water the gardens.

Sg 8:13

3. In this crowded gathering,³ are there not as many gardens as there are spirits? Through unity in spirit there is one garden; through different graces there are many gardens. In these gardens may 'no root of bitterness' raise its head;* may there exist no worthless tree, nothing which ill becomes the garden of the bride. May there be no garden of greens here for 'green herbs will quickly wither'. 'Let him who is weak eat green herbs', says Paul.⁴ But you do not need green herbs, as if you were weak. For what is weak in you is stronger than in people of the world. Their weakness finds rest in what is lawful; yours toils towards what is perfect. Their weakness is to rely on what is allowed; yours to stop just short of what is perfect. For you what else is it to be weak, but to be less than perfect? For you what else is it to be weak but not to reach the summit of perfection? And what is it to be strong, but to strive to reach the summit?

Heb 12:15

Therefore our weakness is stronger than weakness in people of the world and, I may say, better is the weakness of a monk than of a person of the world who behaves well.⁵ How great would deeds be considered which among us are regarded as weak, if such deeds were seen performed by them? Solid food is for the perfect; yet whoever among us is imperfect disdains a diet of green vegetables. What is lawful for the weak of the world is neither set before us nor demanded by us. What we profess is perfect, even if its execution be weak. What we plant is perfect, though its growth be feeble. Our plants must be watered that they may grow but with waters of the spirit. Paul knew well with what waters to irrigate each garden. To married folk he allows the use of marital intercourse;* the fainthearted he encourages, the weak he helps;* to those still of the flesh he gives milk to drink;* he speaks of wisdom to the spiritual who judge all things, a wisdom however not of this world but from God, wisdom hidden in mystery.*

And if anyone else speaks of the 'beauty of the Lord, the place where his glory dwells',* the delights of the bridal chamber, the joy with which the Bridegroom rejoices over the bride and with which in turn she rejoices in the Lord, obviously he ought not to irrigate a vegetable garden with such waters. Indeed 'the unspiritual man does not receive the gifts of the Spirit of God'.* And in general, does not anyone who either gives spiritual directives for action or sets forth spiritual principles for the understanding seem to you to overflow like an unsullied fountain in aromatic gardens? Truly he is unsullied, for thanks to the perfection of his hearers who harken in gardens, he needs only to discuss the purity of spiritual life and, as it were, to lead the occupants of paradise to drink from the streams of paradise.

4. In this interpretation, take the garden to be the hearers, the fountain the teachers. But if teachers are a fountain, how are they a well? Now you know how different from each other are the fountains and the wells of our experience. A well is dug; a fountain flows of its own accord. In a well waters are stored; from a fountain waters emerge, even presenting themselves unsought. Great is the difference between them, nor can the qualities of one be found in the other interchangeably. A fountain cannot claim the distinctive features of a well or a well those of a fountain; each is confined to the limits of its own nature. On earth our physical sources of water are limited but resources of the spirit bubble over. If

we refer our sources of water to resources of the spirit, it will be possible to find a fountain and a well in the same person and the qualities of each source shared with the other.

Let us then communicate the qualities of each one to the other if you wish and in one person let us point out both qualities. In the fountain let us recognize a sufficiency of doctrine, in the well its hidden nature; in the fountain abundance, in the well deep mysteries. Yes indeed, he is a good teacher who as from a deep well so from a hidden treasure of wisdom 'provides wealth new and old'.* He is a well, because 'the thoughts of God no one comprehends except the Spirit of God'. 'For the Spirit searches everything, even the depths of God',* and like a fountain he brings everything out into the open to irrigate the gardens of the virtues.* So in the well you have hiddenness, in the fountain abundance; profusion in the fountain and profundity of meaning in the well. Here is a deep well which requires no bucket, a fountain which flows freely. 'If anyone thirsts, let him come and drink'* of the waters of the bride, of the waters of Beersheba, that a new Solomon may be born of her fountain. Now Beersheba means the 'seventh well',[6] that is, the well of repose, the well of wisdom. For in the list of spiritual gifts wisdom comes in the seventh place in ascending order.[7]

    Mt 13:52

    1 Co 2:11, 10

    Is 58:11

    Jn 7:37

5. As the well of wisdom is mentioned so also is the fountain of wisdom.* And perhaps in these two sources twin channels of wisdom are indicated: one which occurs through investigation, the other through inspiration. The waters of a fountain break out without priming, but in a well the mass of earth is broken through and its solidity penetrated that you may reach living water. Each is necessary to the other, industry to grace and grace to industry, and they offer each other mutual help. For the well-digger toils in vain, if the fountain of life does not flow without priming. But you will have dug yourself a well and prepared a reservoir for water to no purpose, if your well has been abandoned and clogged

    Si 1:5

with silt; living waters will not descend into it, they 'will not flow in a torrent from Lebanon'.* The waters which cascade from Lebanon can be channeled only into a clean well and waters which flow in a torrent long for a capacious well. You will make the well of your heart deep and capacious if you remove earthly cares, if you prepare a place in your spirit for spiritual joy, if you open your mouth to draw in the spirit and if streams of living water flow into your heart.*

For this work 'your settings were prepared on the day of your birth', as Ezechiel wrote of the King of Tyre.* The capacity for natural intelligence, with which on the day of your creation you were privileged above other living creatures, serves in place of a vast reservoir for receiving and holding the waters of vision and of life. Indeed we read of the well of the Living and All-seeing One.* If after sin, however, your well appears to be obstructed by vices either inborn or acquired, let faith clear it, let hope constantly dig deep into it, let love expand it. Let leisure and freedom from preoccupation not allow it to be blocked with filthy silt. For festive joys demand minds free from anxious cares and the vision of God claims leisure for its exercise.[8] Does he not seem to you to be a deep well, 'in whom are hidden all the treasures of the wisdom and the knowledge of God'?* Will you deny that Mary was like a well of purest water, for she 'stored all the words' which concerned Christ 'pondering them in her heart'?* Do you also be such a well according to your capacity, a well deep and full.

6. Having abandoned the wells of Quarrel and of Accusations, Isaac dug two more: the well of Expanse and the well of Plenty.* In the former he began no longer to contend with vices; in the latter he began to delight in the fruit of virtue. He was unwilling to share a well with the Philistines, whose name means 'Falling in their Drink'. To the Philistines he abandoned the wells of Quarrel and Accusations. They fall prostrate, of course, who drink from the well of error and schism. Their authors dig for their

adherents to drink from such wells. So did Arius dig, so did Donatus. The one brought Quarrel into the faith, the other broke into factions the bond of brotherhood. Arius, by his heretical definition, introduced degrees into the equality of the Trinity; Donatus, by his presumption, divided into factions the unity of the Church.[9] Dathan and Abiram dug wells of Quarrel against Moses and Aaron, and themselves fell into the pit which they had made, for the earth swallowed them alive.* They fell headlong thanks to the drink for which they themselves had dug, illustrating by the result the name of the Philistines. *Nb 16*

But good is the well, when the man who drinks of its water will lift up his head* and not stumble after the drink. He digs a pit for himself, who bores into the solid ground of Scripture with the keenness of his earthly understanding and violently scatters the little garden of the Church, producing some unheard of dogma and obscure mysteries. So does the man who by subtle scrutiny and wily scheming bores into the solid wall of brotherly love and discloses a vein of discord, who encloses and seals himself in the well of plots, not consenting to emerge but sinking deeper and deeper into the cavern of schism and excavating its depth. *Ps 109:7*

This is the well of the Philistines; have nothing to do with it. Imperceptibly at first and secretly the waters rise and seep from the pit of an earthy and sensuous mind,* until afterwards they tumble like rapids; but they do not flow from Lebanon. These waters are not reliable;* they are not living waters. Discord cannot remain in harmony; among those who beget schism lasting peace cannot be maintained. Schism is disloyal to itself; it cannot hold together very long because it strives to break up the cement of charity. If anyone should invite you to these wells, wreck if you can the wells of the Philistines and drain dry their pestilential waters; abandon to the Philistines their wells, their wells of Accuasations. *1 Co 15:47; Jm 3:15* *Is 33:16*

7. Search for wells of heavenly delights, the wells

of reliable waters and of living waters, which flow in a 'torrent from Lebanon'.* Be a blossom of the garden, of the garden enclosed, that you may not be plucked, and you will see how the Lord will open fountains and torrents for you.* Live your life in the garden in the hope that you may be changed into a well and from your bosom 'will flow streams of living water'.* What are living waters but waters which never fail?* Good indeed are the waters, a draught of which slakes without fail the thirst of desire. The allurements of world without exception exhibit a false appearance of refreshment and allay worldly concupiscence only for a moment. As suddenly as they rise, so suddenly they recede and fail to flow in a continuous channel. Like a flash flood they suddenly subside and after the flood it is impossible to find living waters.

 Isaac dug in a river bed of a different kind and found living waters. For there is a flood which seems sweet but is neither wholesome nor everlasting, like the worldly flow of pleasure we mentioned above. Again there is a flood which is wholesome but not everlasting, and yet if you dig in it you will find living waters. 'We have confirmation of what was spoken in prophecies,' says Peter. 'You will do well to depend on prophecy as on a lamp for lighting a way through the dark, until the day dawns and the morning star rises in your hearts.'* This lamp will not be extinguished in our darkness, for in the meantime it is needed for our use. But when eternal day dawns, the lamp of prophetic teaching will end and the flood of written speech will run dry.[10] Now 'as for prophecies, they will pass away; as for tongues, they will be silent; as for knowledge, it will disintegrate'.*

 By comparison with the revelation to come, the word of sacred Scripture, so to speak, like a flash flood flows past with murky water, instructing us as if 'in a mirror and in riddles'.* But the waters of that wisdom which is 'face to face'* are true, pure and everlasting. They will not fail you nor you them. When the flash flood of our mortality has passed, with our mortality will pass the mists of mysteries, and without fog the sparkling waters of the truth for which we had dug here in our riverbed will merrily well up. Here is the place to look at truth in a mirror, but there to look truth in the eye.[11] Yet to some extent that direct vision of truth invades our foreign soil and, merrily presenting itself to travellers in a place of pilgrimage, invites us to our fatherland. Indeed both the ray of that eternal light and the stream of that eternal river, however festive, are to us still furtive. That ray does not twinkle, that stream does not sparkle, except in gardens, in gardens of perfume. 'O depth of the riches of the wisdom and knowledge of God',* how you resemble a well! You cannot be exhausted; you pour forth living waters, waters wholesome and bountiful.   *Rm 11:33*

8. Who will give my little garden these waters and my heart this well of delights? 'From my hidden faults cleanse me, Lord, and from sins not my own spare your servant.'* Make me a Lebanon! 'Sprinkle me and I shall be clean; wash me and I shall be brighter than snow.'* 'Cleanse me from the greatest sin and the words of my mouth will be agreeable and the meditation of my heart always in your sight.'* Make me a Lebanon, that I may ever pour forth these waters for you. 'They will be agreeable,' says the psalm. What does 'agreeable' mean but that each of two actions will please and will please each of two persons. Who are the two persons but You and I? What are the two actions but my words of praise and my heart's meditation? These are living waters, because they are ever pleasing, ever flowing, but they flow only from Lebanon, and not in a trickle but in a torrent.   *Ps 18:13-14* *Ps 50:19* *Ps 18:14-15*

A mighty torrent is the experience of passionate love, yet its approaches are gentle, not steep. Mighty is the rush of its torrent, for without let or hindrance it flows right into our affections and gently ebbs away with them. Mighty is its torrents for nothing can check its passion. 'With a torrent from Lebanon'; by naming Lebanon, our text has expressed the reason for its overflow. Purity is the place of overflowing gladness and it pours out waters of saving wisdom; the waters burst from what is bright and make it brighter.

Gather together and, as it were, heap in one pile these delights. Behold and consider the well, Lebanon, the torrent, the living waters. Herein you will detect, if you observe in spirit, that these waters are calm and hidden and powerful and unfailing. The well denotes hiddenness, Lebanon calmness. In the torrent all other affection is exhausted; the living waters cannot be exhausted. A good Lebanon also is faith, because by faith hearts are purified.* From this Lebanon of calm understanding living waters flow; for unless you believe you will not understand.* But good is the understanding when its contemplation remains for ever and ever; this understanding is really alive, for this is eternal life that we should know the one true God and Jesus Christ whom He has sent.* And Christ himself is our Lebanon, pouring living delights in a torrent into the bosom of his beloved. He is the Lebanon and he is the stream, since he is the brightness of eternal life and the purest outpouring. A delightful well assuredly is the bride's affection, into which the rays of eternal brightness, like streams from Lebanon, are both collected and poured out, that they may water the flowers and gardens of the Bridegroom. Good is the Lebanon, then, into which nothing defiled makes its way and mighty is the torrent which cannot be checked by any obstacle.

9. In Paul's words, the waters flow in a torrent into the one whom neither persecution, nor hunger, nor peril, nor nakedness, nor the sword can separate from the love of Christ.* Among believing peoples, though so many stumbling blocks of scandal have been cast in the way and so many monstrous tortures have barred the way, still the waters ever flow from Lebanon. Indeed the waters are the peoples.* Great are the obstacles but greater is the torrent. If you should try to check it, it increases the more and breaks through the barriers. If dammed up, it rises to a crest and, gaining momentum from opposition, overflows more bountifully. For pure love even the very obstacles towards good,* and virtue under

provocation increases in value.

If I keep silence, cannot these provocations shake the consciences* of those whose love flows in unpredictable places and times, who love for a season but in the season of trial fall away?* Why do I 'trial'? Even if they suffer not the burden but the mere obstacle of a slight and doubtful temptation, they are easily checked and abandoning their resolution rush back to the world with a force nothing can halt. If you cry after them in the words of the prophet: 'Stay, stay',* not one of them returns. No persuasion calls them back,* not the devoted pursuit of a teacher, not the unhappiness which often and almost always turns up along their ways.* They scatter and rush and stumble, to drink by the wayside from the torrent of pleasure, which will not raise but shatter their heads upon the earth.* 'Blessed indeed are the spotless on their way, who walk in the law' of charity,* who walk in the torrent, wherever the torrent of the Spirit leads.* They do not retreat or become separated by any obstacle from the love of God,* which is in Christ Jesus our Lord, who lives and reigns for ever and ever. Amen.

1 Co 8:12

Sir 37:4; Mk 4:17

Na 2:8
Ga 5:8

Ps 13:3; Rm 3:16

Ps 109:6-7

Ps 118:1
Ezk 1:12

Rm 8:33, 39

NOTES TO SERMON THIRTY-SEVEN

1.   G. writes to one individual, except in par. 4, *nostis . . . vultis . . . habetis.*
2.   *Copiosi ex hoc fonte rivuli gratiarum emanant, et semper tamen fons manet.* The Latin word-play *emanant . . . manet* is frequent.
3.   *Frequenti conventu.* See Lam 15, n. 58; 19, nn. 82, 83.
4.   Paul and Gilbert here lack neither good sense nor good humor. As the Jerusalem Bible comments on Rm 14:2: 'Christians not sufficiently instructed in the faith and therefore without the firm convictions that would give them a sure conscience, vv. 2, 5, 22, considered themselves bound to observe certain days, v. 5, and to abstain from meat or from wine, vv. 2, 21, perhaps as a permanent obligation, v. 21. Such ascetical practices were familiar to the pagan world (the Pythagoreans) and the Jewish (the Essenes, John the Baptist). Paul lays down the same general rule as in the similar case of 1 Co 8; 10:14-13: each must "act for the Lord" as his conscience tells him, vv. 5-6, provided it is not a doubtful conscience, v. 23; but above all, charity must govern the conduct of those "strong" in the faith, vv. 1, 15, 19-21 and 15:1-13.' The early Cistercians would have especially appreciated G.'s good humor, for they were strict vegetarians, abstaining from meat, fowl, eggs and fish at all times, and from milk products including cheese and butter during long months of the year. The monks of *Notre Dame des Prairies* point out that though *olus* does not appear in RB, the pertinent passage, RB 39:1-5, is neatly summed up in the third stanza of the hymn for All Saints of the Order, *Avete Solitudinis:*
Vobis olus cibaria | Fuere vel legumina!
Your daily food was beans | Or vegetable greens.
5.   See Lam 41, with allusion to Si 42:14, and comparison with Bernard SC 12:9, I 66:6-21, and QH 4:3 and 7:14, PL 183: 184A and 184D.
6.   Gn 21:30-31; Leclercq, 'Otia Monastica', 120:29.
7.   Is 11:1-9; Rm 12:8; reading *sapientia* with Mss and Mab. for *sapientiae* of Migne.
8.   Leclercq, 'Otia Monastica', 91:35.
9.   See *Church History,* by Karl Bihlmeyer, rev. Hermann Tüchle, tr. Victor E. Mills (Westminster, Md.: Newman, 1958) on Arius, I, pp. 246-56, on Donatus, I, pp. 264-7. See C.H. Talbot, "Sermones Inediti B. Aelredi Abbatis Rievallensis", Rome: 1952, Intro. pp. 20-23.
10.   *literarius sermo,* an apt title for the literary genre of G.
11.   See J. Chatillon, 'Hic, ibi, interim', RAM 25 (1949) 194-99.

SERMON 38
WINTRY NORTH AND WARM SOUTH WINDS

Within and without, the lover is affected by north and south winds. 1. Gilbert laments the disasters of his day. 2. Scarcity within and oppression without crush the monks but even more their abbot. 3. The ebb and flow of temptation and consolation existed even among the apostles. 4. Persecution, as in the early Church, can be salutary. 5. The north wind within us is tedium and sadness. 6. This is harmless if we are not responsible. 7. Pray to the Lord for those so afflicted.

BEGONE, O NORTH WIND, AND COME, O SOUTH WIND, BLOW THROUGH MY GARDEN, AND LET ITS PERFUMES FILL THE AIR*[1] Sg 4:16

Sweet and holy affections are the perfumes of the bride. For she is his garden. When the south wind blows, her perfumes are diffused for the delights of the Bridegroom but in turn the inclemency of the north wind stops their flow. Chilling is the north wind and when it blows, her perfumes are frozen. How long, O Lord, will the north wind of adversity oppress our regions? How long will it brood over our little gardens? How long, good Jesus, will the frost of the north wind congeal our perfumes? Spare, O Lord, spare your bride from the north wind. Long has its raw and violent blast been driving and oppressing and brooding. From all sides mounting adversity overwhelms us. Command the wind, Lord, to rise and be gone, to allow us to catch our breath.

The impoverishment of misfortune is barren or everywhere begets serious disasters. Slender resources are easily harmed and one abyss of misfortune calls to another with the roar of your cataracts.* Do you secretly mount attacks against us,* as if you were saying to the north wind: attack, oppress, plunder? 'Smoke will come from the north,' says Isaiah.* But not smoke so much as a flame threatens us now, the flame of a cauldron aboil from the blast of the north wind.* From the north comes frost and from the north comes flame. So it is, O Lord. 'In the harshness of your hand you oppose me';* you check the streams of your mercy. Therefore my spirit burns and in my meditation fire will break out.* Burdensome is this fire of fretful worry and in its heart perfumes do not spread but rather, if you allow any perfumes to spread, their flow is dried up, especially when an opening for misfortunes seems more and more to confront us.

2. *Lord, my sorrow is in your sight and 'my lament is not hidden from you'.** Known to you is the reason for my anxiety. I should rather have said for my grief, for all my anxiety now has begun to pass into grief. Where no ray of good counsel breaks through, where even a shadow of fair hope does not appear, there one plays the role not of anxiety but of grief. My groans multiply and my heart grieves. Little ones beg for bread and there is no one to break it for them,* for there is none to be broken. I do not mean the bread of the word but this daily food for the body. Yet my soul cannot be filled with the richness of that heavenly bread as long as lack of this daily bread brings on, as it were, the emaciation of grief. Distracted by the sound of their sobbing, I have forgotten to eat that heavenly bread.

A harsh north wind is exterior hardship, but much harsher is anxiety of mind. One of the two overburdens you, brethren; both together oppress me. I carry a burden among you because of our common distress and a distress of my own beyond yours,

---

Marginal references:
Ps 41:8
Jr 9:7-9
Is 14:31
Jr 1:13
Jb 30:21
Jr 20:9

Ps 37:18, 10

Lm 4:4, Lam 175, n. 28

because it is on your behalf. Hence arise cases of misfortune, hence legal quarrels. Some whisper, others taunt, and what is beyond human effort to prevent from happening, they turn into a reproach when it happens. Some provoke, others mock, attributing bad luck to folly. Good results in which they rejoice, they ascribe to themselves and consider the fruit of their foresight or merit, not of God's bounty. 'The tents of brigands thrive,' says Job, 'and brashly they challenge God, although he has placed everything in their hands.'* Some are both brigands and braggarts, for what belongs to God they filch for themselves in assigning it to themselves; they attribute the gift of God's grace to the effectiveness of their own effort.[2] Why do you reproach us with the blessings dispensed to you from on high? Because the eye of divine clemency looks kindly upon you, must your eye look askance at us? Why do God's blessings make you more ready to depreciate than to appreciate?   Jb 12:6

3. *You see, O Lord, on how many sides blasts from the north wind assail us. From all sides troubles, murmuring, reproaches blow upon us. Distracted and hampered amid such sorrows, the spirit cannot welcome the gentle breezes of the south wind. Arise, O Lord; let not the north wind prevail; long enough now has it been rioting and swooping upon us; command it to rise and be gone and yield to the south wind. The cauldron has been boiling now for a long while before the face of the north wind,* but do you dispatch the south wind, O Lord, to make the center of this forge like a breeze fresh as dew. I dare not ask for uninterrupted breezes from the south; it is enough if the inclemency of the north wind be moderated even by some alternation with the south. You stretch the north wind over the void, as we read in Job,* not over your garden.*   Jr 1:13

Jb 26:7

The little garden of the bride is not empty, for in it have been planted all the perfumed species listed above. And how will the glad perfumes of meditation be able to flow where our studies are not free from grief, where hardship saddens and the north wind binds? Be a zealot, Lord,* be jealous over the bride, command the north wind to abate and with the south wind to share equal seasons. This will happen, if to match the great number of sorrows in my heart, your consolations bring joy to my soul. You see, brethren, how the north wind might give birth to the south in its own measure and perhaps where the north wind has abounded, the south wind will abound even more. For the south wind will both blow favorably and compensate for the damage the north wind has inflicted. Therefore let the north wind arise, let it rage and bluster to its heart's content, provided it offers an entrance and an opening³ to the breezes of the south.

Do they not seem to you to have endured the bluster of the north wind, whom Paul addresses in the Epistle to the Hebrews: 'You endured a hard struggle with sufferings,' he says, 'sometimes being publicly exposed to abuse and affliction, and sometimes being partners with those so treated. For you had compassion on the prisoners.'* But amid such blasts of the north wind did not the south wind claim its turn? Indeed it did. In Paul, hear what follows: 'And you joyfully accepted the plundering of your property, since you knew that you yourselves had a better possession and an abiding one.'* Again when the apostles 'left the presence of the Council, rejoicing because they had been found worthy to suffer outrage for the name' of Jesus,* does not the south wind seem to you to have breathed gently upon them after the driving attacks of the north?

Consider that sad Sabbath when the Lord lay in the tomb. Did the hearts of the apostles not shiver in disbelief and timidity, as if before the blast of the north wind? At the Resurrection of the Lord, a gentle south wind began to blow through his garden. As Scripture shows, throughout these forty days, from many proofs of his Resurrection, both belief in his truth and confidence in his liberation gradually increased. On the very day of Pentecost, when there came a mighty wind into the upper room 'where the apostles were sitting',* all the chill of their minds thawed 'like an inundation in the south',* and henceforth the fragrance of their word and their virtues filled the air.

4. But for all that, did the harsh north wind keep its peace? Did not the storm of the persecutors and the blast of heretical tempests arise much more violently? Did not the north wind of temptation in jealous rivalry fall upon the south wind of grace? Like a lone survivor, the north wind attempts to blow through the garden with the chill of its harsh blast, trying to prevent perfumes from filling the air. But so much the further is the perfume carried. Now stimulated, now lulled in alternate waves of adversity and prosperity, the bride of Christ, his Church, did not then and does not now cease to diffuse the perfume of virtues. In persecution her courage shone bright; in peace her numbers increased. In persecution the valiant are tested, in peace the weak are strengthened.

Yet why do I now recall the primitive Church, when the Bridegroom's garden still encounters frequent though not so violent assaults of the north wind? The sound and the north winds take turns in the garden. In our time a great tempest is driving the Church and indeed from the north.[9] For from there the schism originates, from there it rises and there it lingers; from there like a lone survivor the north wind is her oppressor. Command it, Lord, to rise and be gone. Summon the south wind and say: 'Come, blow through my garden, let its perfumes fill the air.' I do not mean the south wind of earthly happiness and security, for this south wind often checks and dries up the perfumes; but summon the south wind of your grace. And if need be, send the north wind also into that barren garden, the north wind not of stubbornness but of trial, that trial itself may grant understanding to obey when we hear your command.* Lash your garden with the chill north wind; as if with blows, rouse it from sloth, that it may turn more eagerly to the gentle gusts of the south wind. Not only in different seasons but also in different regions, the south and north winds blow by

Ps 125:4

Is 28:19

turns in her garden. Just as now the south wind blows and then the north, so here the south blows and there the north. Sometimes however both blow together, but the one outside and the other inside, the north wind outside and the south inside, the former raging, the latter assuaging. Let the north wind bluster and riot outside; only let it not blow through the garden inside, let it not penetrate within, let it not choke the interior gladness of the heart which is in Christ.

When, O Lord, will that freezing wind subside altogether? When will come the time with no further fear of its frosty face? Your city has been founded, your garden planted on the northern slopes. This wind in Scripture is said to be on the right. That is why Job utters such a complaint about it: 'At the right hand of the East my troubles rose up at once.'*[5] *Justifiably he called that wind 'on his right', since it could not bring him anything sinister!*[6] *Rather it brought the righteous man an increase of glory, when his courage, once tested, shone bright and, once challenged, was increased. From close by, this wind swoops into your garden, for your garden lies on the northern slopes. Make this wind favorable to us, O Lord; moderate it with the breezes of the south wind. For even the north wind cooperates with us for the blessing of your love, when the south wind also blows. Whether it arises at your bidding or by your permission, let not the north wind of trial make us afraid. For in a little while the south wind of consolation will follow on its heels, even if in the meantime the south wind does not intervene. Indeed where affliction abounded, grace also abounded.**

5. But why do I talk to you, brethren, about outward trial? A different north wind is wont to molest you. God spares you this outward north wind, interposing other men to bear the brunt of the frequent assaults of worldly turmoil and trial. No burdensome outward anxiety ties you in knots, because by right none touches you; yet anxiety does not leave you immune.* Those whom outward anxiety cannot affect, inner anxiety afflicts with

boredom. Things go well with them in one region because they are not exposed to outward activities. But none the less they do not escape the north wind, when they are not satisfied with themselves in interior activities. Joys once festive turn to disdain and sadness transforms the cheerful face of the mind.

Happy the man who does not experience this transformation. But who is he? Who is the man whom boredom does not weary at times and sadness exasperate? According to Acts, where we were making headway with fair sailing, there shortly afterwards we run into shallows and over those sailing with a fair wind an opposing gale breaks.* Even when no reason is apparent, trouble intrudes. Since its source is not evident, it poses a threat. A man is angry at the anger he suffers without reason, and he loathes the emotion without knowing its source. This harsh spirit breathes where it wills and you know not whence it comes and perhaps where it goes or rather where it ends.⁷ For of itself such an emotion goes towards evil, but often it results in good. It does not reach the goal to which it tends but 'God provides a way out even of trial'.* When he wishes he introduces the north wind; when he wishes he commands: 'North wind, begone!' *Ac 27:13-26* *1 Co 10:13*

If in the meantime you complain of its annoyance, know that thanks to such teaching you are given a reminder and a warning. You are reminded to be aware of the nearness of the north wind, warned to avoid its chill. It is not in your power to escape its neighborhood as long as you dwell on the northern slopes, but you can escape its violence. While we are here, the north wind is always our neighbor. It is not always violent, but after we have wheeled through the north, we often tack back by the south.* Even when you do not feel its assault, be on guard against its proximity. *Qo 1:6*

6. Yet when will you escape its whirlwind, unless the gentle south wind comes when called, and so you may spread your wings to the south wind and grow feathers for the flight to heaven?* If however the north wind strives to intervene and with freezing *Jb 39:36*

blast to check the new growth of your wings, it does hamper your wings from flight and your perfume from filling the air. It hampers, I admit, but does not blow your wings away. Yes, utter boredom and bitterness of heart exercises the virtues without destroying them. This whirlwind attacks your holy resolve without blowing it away. It checks your happiness; it does not blow your constancy away.

The spirit is affected by boredom but is not overwhelmed. The spirit is saddened but wrestles with its sadness. Virtue thus troubled is not less brave but less happy. What has the spirit in common with the vice with which it brawls, against which it declares war? The spirit is not responsible for the disgust it feels, since it never came to terms with disgust. The spirit suffers assault but does not surrender. According to our text, the spirit itself does not initiate this struggle but rather the north wind, on whose slopes it dwells. So the spirit loathes this disgust, feeling its batteries aimed at virtue.

The spirit attacked by boredom knows with what boredom it endures being bored with the good life, how it disdains the disdain, with what bitterness it wrestles against bitterness, against that violent bitterness which intrudes uninvited into the unchanging round of regular discipline. The spirit by choice veers towards the south wind and behold! the north wind relentlessly interferes, despite the vigorous opposition óf the spirit. It is hard to hold out against that frosty face and it is not in our power to break its hold. The spirit is worn out both by its boredom with discipline and by loathing for this boredom. Both feelings are repugnant: to have no taste for what you have chosen and to experience what you loathe. Each is a trial: to protect discipline and to put lethargy to rout.[8]

7. *How do you tolerate for so long, good Jesus, so much harassment of your beloved bride? Unwillingly she suffers lethargy and pursues it to punish it in herself as if it were deliberate. She scarcely endures her inability to delight at will in you who are her only good. She blames herself for what she*

suffers unwillingly. One comes from the north wind to goad her, but his goad spurs the bride to prayer. Chafed by this goad she casts herself on her knees, though previously she had made ready for your embraces.⁹ Protect your bride, good Jesus, from these evil days. For unless you help her, her soul will dwell in the north wind. Who will rise against the north wind but you, O God, who come from the south? A good perfume is holy resolution and a pure conscience, but it does not surround a spirit which fails to enjoy the delights of your blessing. Come, good Jesus, come; blow through your garden that its perfumes may flow 'like an overflow in the south'.* Ps 125:4
Your bride is the garden; do you be the south wind. When you water it, her soul will be like a well watered garden* and when you blow, her perfumes Jr 21:12 will not fail, for you live and reign for ever and ever. Amen.

NOTES ON SERMON THIRTY-EIGHT

1. G. writes to one individual, but note *fratres* in par. 2, *Videtis, fratres,* in par. 3, *vobis, fratres . . . vos,* in par. 5.
2. Reading *effectum* with mss and Migne for *affectum* of Mab.
3. Reading *materiam* with mss rather than *quasi vim* preferred by Mab. and Migne.
4. Sermon 41 was delivered shortly after the death of Aelred of Rievaulx, 11 January 1167, so that one may suppose that Sermon 38 was composed not long before that date. The north wind and the schism here may thinly disguise the quarrel between Henry II and Thomas à Becket. The quarrel hardened with Becket's successful resistance to Henry's attempt to make 'an illegal appropriation of money,' in July 1163 (Mann, X:161). 'This is . . . the first case of any opposition to the King's will in the matter of taxation which is recorded in our national history.' (Stubbs, *Constitutional History of England,* I:463, quoted in Mann.) After what became known as the Constitution of Clarendon (January 1164) and the Council of Northampton (October 1164) Becket escaped to the continent, and from November, 1164 was living at the great Cistercian Abbey of Pontigny. See L. A. Desmond, 'Becket and the Cistercians,' *Canadian Catholic Historical Association* 35 (1968) 9-29.
5. See de Lubac, *Exégèse,* 2:411.
6. G. plays on the word 'sinister', which also means 'left'.
7. *An magis quo evadat?* This is the second half of a double indirect question. Lam 197, n. 179.
8. Lam 170, nn. 3, 4; 197, n. 180.
9. Lam 188, n. 120, referring not to S 33:7, but to S 38:7.

SERMON 39
FREEDOM, AFFECTIVITY, AND GRACE

The lover distinguishes freedom, affectivity and grace: 1. Fear is opposed to a good resolution. 2. The spirit of slavery differs from the spirit of freedom. 3. Freedom of choice contributes nothing, if grace is absent; Gilbert discusses freedom of choice. 4. Freedom is not withdrawn in the state of fallen nature; Gilbert distinguishes freedom of our state, of disposition, of affection. 5. Freedom to will the good freely is distinguished from freedom to will the good affectively. 6. All things flow gently and fruitfully from charity and knowledge.

BEGONE, O NORTH WIND, AND COME, O SOUTH WIND, BLOW THROUGH MY GARDEN AND LET ITS PERFUMES FILL THE AIR*[1]   Sg 4:16

Execute your command, good Jesus; dispatch the south wind from heaven and conduct it into your garden, into the soul of your bride. By this gentle breeze dispel boredom, dispel sadness from her feelings. For each is a misery and each resembles the north wind; each fetters the mind, as it were, bars access to the current of pure joy. What is the effect of fear? With its chilling harshness does fear not also constrain the affection? Spare your bride, Lord, from feelings not her own. What is more alien to her than a fear which does not exist in charity, since the bride's whole existence is in charity? Fear is enslaving; she has been *called to freedom.*

You saw, brethren, in yesterday's sermon,[2] a man proceed fearfully in order to undergo the first elements of formation. With what a slow and stumbling resolve he allowed himself to become initiated into the rudiments of discipline! You know well what generous streams of alms his hands poured out, while he was still a man of the world. What made him hesitate but the north wind of fear in our region, which paralyzed his mind? The south wind, of course, had blown upon part of his mind but did not blow through it; therefore he was quick to scatter abroad the fragrance of almsgiving, but after many efforts at long last scarcely a trickle of that most precious and fragrant perfume of renunciation could be squeezed from his spirit. Obviously he resembled the young man in the Gospel who, having boasted to the Lord of his observances of the Law, when the narrow way of evangelical perfection was set before him, went away sad;* with this difference: the man in Matthew went away sad while our man, although sad, came forward none the less.

Notice the north wind of fear blowing under the Law; therefore few of the precious and choice perfumes filled the air under the Law. But on the day of Pentecost, when the Spirit blew mightily from the south, so many thousands of men poured forward in the truth, in the word and in the life of the Spirit.* Care for their private affairs did not shackle them for the future.

2. Hearts free from this truly harsh north wind pour themselves out more generously in contemplation and in love of God. 'You did not receive,' says Paul, 'the spirit of slavery to fall back into fear, but you received the spirit of sonship in which we cry: "Abba, Father".'* The former was the spirit of the north wind, the latter of the south; the north grievous, the south gracious. Therefore the bride bids the north wind 'begone', because it is grievous and burdensome and oppressive, but the south wind, joyful and agreeable, is invited to come and blow through the little garden of the Bridegroom.

The north wind brings torture, the south brings rippling laughter. The north is a menace, the south brings waves of caresses and delights. 'I will ask my Father,' says the Lord, 'and he will give you another Paraclete';* this is to invite the south wind and bid it come blow through his garden. 'Blow through my garden and let its perfumes fill the air.' *Jn 14:16*

Some fruits do not pour out their juices unless they are squeezed and crushed. But fruits which exist in a garden so delicately described do not wait to be squeezed; they cannot be crushed, but when the south wind blows they pour out their juices gratuitously. Look at the wisdom of the world. Does it not seem to be violently squeezed out and developed by long practice and study? But in the authors of our philosophy the depths of wisdom surge up both speedily and powerfully. Would you hear of its speed? 'When you stand before kings and governors do not think beforehand; it will be given you in that hour, what you should speak.'* Would you hear of its power? 'I will give you a mouth and wisdom which none of your adversaries will be able to withstand.'* How would these words flow so suddenly and so calmly, if the south wind did not blow? You have heard now whence come the perfumes of truth, so plentiful and so apt for the occasion. *Mt 10:18-19; Mk 9:11* *Lk 21:15*

3. Has not charity likewise 'been poured into our hearts by the Holy Spirit who has been given to us'?* Many are the perfumes which are poured through the Spirit and only through the Spirit: joy, peace, patience, longsuffering, goodness, kindness, loyalty, meekness, modesty, self-control, chastity.*³ These have not only come forth but have also poured forth. That they pour forth signifies their abundance; that they pour forth at the breath of the south wind signifies the absence of compulsion. Charity cannot be forced; it flows freely. It is borne along not of necessity but by choice, provided the south wind blows. *Lk 21:14-15* *Ga 5:22-23*

For what could the liberty of choice contribute, if the south wind of grace did not blow? Wherever choice exists, choice is always free. But we do not admit that choice is free to choose all things. Choice does not have the liberty to choose or to execute all things. Liberty always exists in making a choice, but it is not always possible to make a choice. Indeed the will can only choose freely, but things do exist which the will cannot choose on its own. The will is its own master, it is free when it is present; but if the will is absent, then the spirit is not free for any act which requires the presence of the will. Nor is the spirit any more its own master because it controls the will it has, or because it has a good will. However, in as far as after the fall the will consists in freedom of choice, the spirit always wills freely what it wills, but the spirit has not been left free to will anything it wishes or even the things it should will.

One freedom exists indeed which does not exist without the will and without which no will exists; but another freedom exists which the will does not always accompany. The former freedom exists in the will, the latter is in some faculty of willing. The former freedom exists in the will, the latter, as it were, is related to the will. The former freedom is in our power but the latter we coerce. So vision is some power of seeing in the eye and at the same time vision is some change which occurs in seeing. So also in the spirit, understanding is called both a natural power to understand and the use of that power.

In choice likewise this distinction occurs; in the same word is expressed both the aptitude and the act. Freedom of choice exists in both, not only in the power to choose but also in the act of choosing; and when the will is exercised in choosing evil, it is always enslaved. The will indeed is enslaved by the very fact that it is weak both for good and against evil. An evil will is free by the very fact that it is a will but enslaved by the very fact that it is evil. For 'everyone who commits sin is the slave of sin'.* Sin ties in knots and binds the one it seizes; sin makes him a captive as long as it coerces him.

4. *But do you, O Lord, 'change our captivity, like a flash flood in the south'.* Send forth your spirit and our primeval freedom will be renewed; it*

will be renewed I say, not created anew. For even if liberty has been obscured, it has not been withdrawn. Liberty remains what it was created to be, but it cannot move itself to what it was created for; it is alive but it does not thrive. So also in madmen their inborn rationality is not lessened but in those so afflicted no movement of reason can thrive. When their great illness has been cured, then reason which was dormant is not given back but is reawakened. So also the liberty of choice congenital to man is neither wholly nor partially withdrawn but is bound fast by sin. It is the same liberty which it was created to be but it has been affected in a different way.

There exist, so to speak, a freedom of our state, a freedom of disposition, and a freedom of affection. The first belongs to our nature and therefore is always good; but unless the first be healed, the second will not aim at goodness or the third exist in goodness. The first consists in a natural aptitude; the second in the habit of a mind which is well or badly constituted; the third consists in actual exercise. Therefore, unless the natural aptitude be assisted by grace, neither the habit of the will nor its actual exercise will look toward virtue. The liberty of choice is weak; so where choice wilts, the south wind will blow and at once perfumes will fill the air. Choice does not have this noble and truly free liberty which exists for goodness and in goodness, unless the Spirit has set it free. *Therefore, O Lord, send forth your Spirit, to bestow through grace both the power to perform and the act of willing, for the Spirit first bestowed the possibility of both when he fashioned human nature.*

We listed three freedoms above: in the third an act of will is present; in the second it is implied; in the first is considered the natural potency directed towards the other two. Therefore let the first be called capacity, the second power, and the third the will. It does not seem to be the same thing to have a natural capacity for something and to have power to perform it. Many things for which we have the capacity by nature, we cannot do at once, when the innate faculty is either hampered by weakness or lacks skills and exercise. Often the eye cannot see for the moment; although vision has not lost its natural capacity; the habit is present but its exercise is absent. By nature the eye is capable of seeing but in fact the eye çannot see. Similarly our natural freedom of choice indeed remains but is hampered by sin, and therefore is unable to have the third freedom which is in goodness, or the second which is toward goodness. The first remains, changed indeed but not diminished; the others must be said not even to remain. For after sin, to will the good is not left free to us, so that our freedom, which consists in a good will, does not remain, but by grace the third freedom is breathed into us, the second is repaired, and the first is created according to nature.

5. Let this much be said of the freedom by which we will the good: that it is from grace. But another freedom exists none the less through grace, by which we not only will rightly but also will goodness itself affectively. The former freedom always exists in the will but the latter does not. Indeed we always will freely but not always affectively. Feelings have nothing to do with our liberty of choice. Yet the freedom of a good will is not wholly free, if it is without affection. But when the south wind blows, at once the perfume of affections fills the air. No pressure is exerted to elicit them; they flow freely. Frequently some boredom and sadness accompany a holy will; but sweet affections do not share the journey with boredom and sadness.*

Affections are a perfume to the sense of smell and equally pleasing to the touch; they are pleasant to experience and pleasant to remember; pleasantly they fill the air and pleasantly they are wafted afar. They fill the air for themselves; they are wafted afar for others. Both are perfumed, affections within and aspirations without. The liberty of choice can aspire to these, but they do not depend on the liberty of choice. As evil feelings often exist despite a good will, so good affections when they are present, even if they exist with a good will, do not flow from it; good will remains free without them and from them,

Lam 197, 178

as it were, breathes freely. Affections make the will itself more free but affections do not flow from freedom of the will. They flow, however, when the south wind blows through.

O gentle south wind, truly desirable, by whose breath the horrid face of winter frost dissolves and the springtime of jocund freshness smiles in gardens, yes, and a new summer and autumnal fruitfulness! Yes, for in the diffusion of perfumes is meant the ripening of harvests. See how good and how pleasant it is to wait in chambers and in gardens for this breath of perfume so fragrant, renewing and recreating the fruits of the Spirit, pouring out its aroma, scattering its bouquets. *Send this Spirit to us, O Lord, to clothe our little garden with a new countenance after the horror of the north wind, and to change our grief into joy.**   Est 13:17.
Lam 18, n. 78.

Or if the north wind means something good, invite it together with the south wind. Let them combine their functions and let each play its part. Let the north wind bind and the south wind loose; let the north tie wantonness in knots and let the south relax the spirit in rippling laughter. Let the north bestow continence and the south make conscience merry. Let the north restrain and the south replenish. 'I have become like a wineskin in the frost,' says the psalmist, 'yet I have not forgotten your statutes.'* Good is the wineskin thus frozen   Ps 118:83
and filled: outside the frost of continence, inside the fulness of righteousness. Well does each wind blow when our exteriors are stiffened as if by the cool wind of continence and our interiors are thawed with overflowing happiness.

6. In order that you may divert the breeze of the south wind to your interior, the bride says 'blow through'. A breeze which blows through, blows into the interior and to it nothing is impenetrable. This breeze is delicate, keen and swift, blowing through without inflating. *Knowledge puffs up;** charity   1 Co 8:1
blows through. Charity is more intimate than knowledge and reaches to more hidden recesses. The Spirit blows through all that is more hidden, for he searches

1 Co 2:10   even the depths of God.* Where he blows through the depths, there the perfumes of knowledge flow for our use: meditations, prayers, sighs, sobs, tears, and colloquies. All fill the air like perfumes for they originate from charity. All things which proceed from charity are fragrant, full of grace. They are precious and abundant, fragrant and filling the air. They overflow because they proceed from the fulness of charity. They overflow and are not squeezed out nor do they suffer the violence of the wine-press. You read of no wine-press built in this garden, for the south wind fulfills the function of the wine-press. What is breathed upon fills the air better than what is trodden upon. For these perfumes, as we said, are gratuitous, not squeezed out through fear but wafted upon the wind.

Some commentators apply the north and the south winds to the adversity and prosperity of this world.[4] And indeed the Church of God, harassed by this twofold temptation, always abounds in the perfumes of good affections and of a good reputation. Hence she endures the necessity of being sifted by these temptations, because she knows how to survive success and how to suffer want. This passage cries for fuller treatment, but in conclusion let it suffice to have touched the topic but lightly. The next sermon will pass on to the mutual invitations of the bride and the Bridegroom, if Jesus Christ who lives and reigns our God, deigns to grant us his grace.

NOTES TO SERMON THIRTY-NINE

1. Gilbert uses plurals of address in par. 1 and 2, the singular in par. 6. See Etienne Gilson, *The Spirit of Mediaeval Philosophy*, (N.Y.: Scribners, 1936) 304-323; D. Odon Lottin, *Psychologie et Morale aux XIIe et XIIIe Siècles*, (Louvain: Abbaye de Mont César, 1942) 1:12-20. In his unpublished dissertation, Lam points out that Gilbert uses the word *arbitrium* but avoids *liberum arbitrium* for liberty is included in the word *arbitrium*; Lam suggests a schema for 'liberty' and its three species, of which the following is an adaptation.

		Libertas	
	1) *conditionis*	2) *dispositionis*	3) *affectus*
relata ad Deum	libertas naturae (libertas arbitrii)	libertas arbitrii & gratia	libertas arbitrii & gratia & affectus
	naturaliter creatur	per gratiam reparatur	per gratiam inspiratur
ad nos	in naturali aptitudine	in habitu bene vel male constitutae mentis	in usu
	potentia	potestas	voluntas
ad bonum	invalida	ad bonum	in bono
	post peccatum, non liberum velle bonum	qua bonum volumus	qua bonum ipsum affectuose volumus

Lam suggests that Gilbert uses St Augustine for his theology of original sin, grace and liberty, and predestination, 'Gilbert of Hoyland' in DSp 6 (1967) 373; Lam finds Gilbert faithful to the thought of Bernard, while changing Bernard's words; see *Sancti Bernardi Opera*, ed. J. Leclercq, H. M. Rochais, (Rome: Ed. Cistercienses, 1963) 3:165-203, *De gratia et libero arbitrio*, and *S. Anselmi Opera Omnia*, ed. F. S. Schmitt, (Edinburgh: Nelson 1946) 1:205-226, *De libertate arbitrii*; see index below (volume 4) under 'choice' and 'liberty'.

2. Probably S 38:5-6; see also 35:2, 7. For 'rudiments of formation', Lam cites 'vigils, fasts, a modest and sparce diet, rough cloth, black bread and strokes of the discipline freely undertaken', S 43:8. Lam 170, nn. 3, 4; 174, n. 22.
3. Lam, 'Gilbert de Hoyland', DSp 6 (1967) 372-3.
4. For such an interpretation, à Lapide, 8:85, quotes Anselm and refers to Richard of St Victor.

SERMON 40
CONTINENCE, REPENTANCE,
AND ALL VIRTUES

The bride bears the fruit of continence, repentance, and of all the virtues. 1. Gilbert's humble confession. 2. False love forgets the absent lover and courts the present, but true love does not act so. 3. Fears for the loss of virginity. 4. The Lord is a passionate lover. 5. He invites from the bride's garden of activity to his own of contemplation. 6. The mystical meanings of myrrh in Christ; chastity differs in Christ, Mary and others; St Lawrence is invited from the gridiron to the garden. 7. Christ's Resurrection is the promise of our own. 8. His Godhead in the flesh is like honey in the honeycomb; gall and vinegar become as sweet as milk and honey.

LET MY BELOVED COME INTO HIS GARDEN TO EAT THE FRUIT OF HIS ORCHARD. COME INTO MY GARDEN, SISTER, MY BRIDE. I HAVE GATHERED MY MYRRH WITH MY SPICES. I HAVE EATEN THE HONEYCOMB WITH MY HONEY; I HAVE DRUNK MY WINE WITH MY MILK*[1]

Sg 5:1

What a gulf exists, brethren, between my behavior and the words which express such desires. The Lord knows my eagerness but I am not rash. Why not be rash? I have no such garden as Christ pictured above, no apples which he eagerly consumes, no fragrant fruits, no gushing fountain, no deep well of living waters. But rather into my garden burst quickly thorns and brambles. *I do not dare, good Jesus, to invite you into such a garden, unless perhaps first to weed, harrow and scatter, and then to plant, and thus in due season you will eat from what your right hand has planted.**²

Ps 79:16

Happy the soul worthy to invite you to fruit already ripe, cultivated fruit without bitterness. Would that bitterness were the only complaint about our fruits! would that they were only unripe, provided they were not bad! Often apples which by nature are good, are not yet tasty because of the season and are only distasteful because unripe. Happy the garden in which all fruits are both good by nature and ready in season. The bride knows that neither quality is lacking in her apples, for to partake of them she entices her Beloved. 'Let my Beloved come into his garden to eat the fruit of his orchard.'

See with what hesitation and modesty and after how many eulogies was her invitation extended. Indeed she does not presume to invite her Beloved, nor does she thirst for delights, until she knows she has been described in quite delicate terms. What do you conclude? Do you think that Jesus grants the delightful coming of his presence to those neither endowed with the qualities mentioned nor worthy of his praises? Consider it a mark of rash presumption to invite Jesus before you are ready for the practise of contemplation. Do you pester him to dally with you, when perhaps you are still grubby with faults? Is your garden still prickly with brambles and becoming barren? And do you invite Jesus there? Invite him not now to dally but to destroy what your right hand has planted. Invite him first to uproot and then to plant. In both there is toil, but with delight he will come to pluck ripe fruit.

2. 'Let my Beloved come,' she cries. Not only does she woo and compliment him in his presence but even in his absence her longing for him is fervent. A false and counterfeit love forgets someone absent but woos someone present. Not so does his bride act,

not so; she longs for him in his absence and rejoices in his presence. 'Let my Beloved come into his garden,' she says. Why does he dispatch the south wind to me? Let him come in person and it is enough for me. He is my south wind, he is my fragrance. He is my south wind, he is my love. 'God comes from the south'* and the south wind comes with him. *Heb 3:3*

According to John, 'he is full of grace and truth'.* Rightly is he my south wind, for he scatters the clouds with his light and gently approaches. My south wind is my Christ. He blows through my garden, he eats my apples. 'Let my Beloved come into his garden, to eat the fruit of his orchard.' The time for pruning has passed; the blossom has given birth to fruit with which it was in labor; winter is gone, spring has vanished, early autumn treads on the heels of departing summer. At last 'let my Beloved come into his garden to eat the fruit of his orchard'. Behold the fulness of time has now come;* therefore 'let my Beloved come into his garden'. The apples have ripened early, therefore 'let him eat the fruit of his orchard. *Jn 1:14*

Ga 4:4

He longs for the first-fruits of the fig tree. Though it was not yet time for figs, he approached a fig tree by the wayside, turned its leaves over and found no fruit.* Before the time for eating and before the time for fruit, he approached it in the morning hungry. For my part I know a fig tree which bore morning fruit from its first childhood, a harvest of firstfruits, fruits of virginal grace. This fig tree was not planted by the wayside but in a garden and in a garden enclosed, in a garden surrounded by the wall of discipline and the thick hedge of custody. Obviously fruitful was this fig tree and among others the most beautiful in appearance. The Lord Jesus often turned aside to it, perhaps adapting her words: 'Beneath the shade of one whom I desired, I sat and the fruit was sweet to my palate.'³ *Mk 11:13*

3. But would that the tree had kept the fruits it produced! Would that the wicked hand of a thief had not deflowered the tree! Now however it has borne its best fruit, and fruit which cannot be reborn. Other

fruit has grown in its place, that is, instead of virginal continence, bitter repentance. With how much greater relish you used to feed both yourself and your Beloved on that natural fruit rather than on this substitute! Woe to you in your misery! When your Beloved shall come, what will be your thoughts, your appearance, your countenance? Where will you turn in your shame, after you have lost the fruits of modesty? Where will you turn? When he shall approach and turn over your leaves and not find the usual fruit, he will blush at your confusion! Recall the words of the vow of virginity; review the words of your consecration. Wait beneath the foliage, since your special fruit no longer exists, the fruit of integrity, the fruit of virginity. Such fruit was consecrated but now it has been plucked.

Consecration and corruption do not sit well together. Violated virginity is wont to be forgiven, though it cannot be given back. 'Glorious tales have been sung about you, O city of God',* but shameful deeds have been done within you. In future, in lamentation acknowledge your role with twofold confusion and shame. 'Who will give water to my head and a fountain of tears to my eyes, and I shall weep'* for the fall not of some woman of the street but as it were, of the foremost in the virginal flock?[4] Who I ask will give me 'a fountain of tears'? For she who has fallen has been wholly dissolved in tears; streams of tears roll down and drench her face. Deep sighs and fretful moans betray what shame, the faithful companion of guilt, tries to hide. In her pitiful face I have seen her downcast look, her furrowed cheeks. Sobs interrupted her words; she would not refrain from falling and could not refrain from tears.

Produce what you are producing, 'the appropriate fruits of repentance'.* Let sorrow renew you; be consumed by grief;* say with the prophet: 'Do not try to console me, I shall weep bitterly.'* I also shall weep with you. Perhaps your Beloved in person will also shed tears with you, since he wept for Lazarus.* Perhaps he weeps even more. His grief is greater, for his love is greater. His mercies are many; 'therefore,'

says the prophet, 'we have not been consumed.'* *Lm 3:22*
In scriptural terms, you are not consumed because he is your counsellor and your consoler, converting your soul.* *Is 9:6; Jb 29:25; Ps 22:3*

To say what almost defies understanding, how will the pitiful face of your grief fail to move his feelings, though in a different way, when I who retrace the course of your sorrow am touched inwardly with heartfelt compassion? If you produce 'the appropriate fruits of repentance', your Beloved will return again into his garden. Yes, gladly he consumes the apples of repentance. Blessed, however, is anyone who guards intact the fruit of original purity. It is good to come to maturity early and in maturity to persevere.

4. Therefore the Bride rises before dawn[5] and says: 'Let my Beloved come into his garden to eat his fruit of his orchard.' 'Come into my garden, sister, my bride.' A passionate lover is the Lord Jesus; at a single word of invitation, he comes flying gladly into the bride's little garden. He flies ahead, as it were, and 'rising before dawn,' cries 'Come'![6] Let this word be taken as an imperative and his cry 'Come!' will suit his actions. He is no dilatory or niggardly rewarder, but without restraint repeats the bride's invitation: 'Come into my garden, sister, my bride. I have gathered my myrrh with my spices.' It is an obdurate affection, which is not moved by such tender invitations and reinvitations! What is more gracious than this interchange? What more surprising than this exchange?

Oh wonderful exchange! The Beloved of God the Father, the glory of heaven, the delight of the angels, allows himself to be invited into our little gardens and does not neglect to invite us to his in return. Even the garden which is ours is more truly called his. For the bride does not say: 'let my Beloved come into *my* garden' but 'into *his* garden'. Rightly 'into his', because given by him and owed to him and certainly dedicated to him. 'Let my Beloved come.' 'Come, sister, my bride.' Great is their tenderness and apt their distinctions. She desires and he commands. She says: 'Let him come'; he answers, 'Come!'

'I stand at the door and knock,' he says. 'If anyone opens to me, I will enter and dine with him and he with me.'* *You have no need to linger, O good Jesus, at the door of the bride, for on her own initiative in her yearning she anticipates you. Reply in kind, invite her in turn. You have sat at her table; notice the quantities set before you, knowing you should prepare for her a repast to match. A repast to match I suggest, and it is enough for her. But I assure you of this: she expends herself without reserve; you should respond in kind. How will it be in kind, if she gives herself fully and you give only half of yourself? A mite of yourself is more than her all. Her all is but a share of your grace; that is why her garden is yours and your garden is hers.*

5. 'Come into my garden.' For my part, brethren, gladly I see in the Bridegroom's garden that abundant and delicate and gloriously planted paradise of Christ's virtues which, in accord with his two natures, he either possessed from eternity or received in time. So, in a parallel, see in the bride's garden the state of the soul or of the Church and the dowry of virtues and affections with which each is enriched by the Bridegroom. In her garden are considered the blessings of the Body, in his garden the blessings of the Head. In both there is beautiful fruit for contemplation. But what is her fruit compared with his? The more the glory of Christ surpasses the virtues either of the soul or of the Church, so much the more delightful is the entrance into his garden.

The active life looks more to the bride's garden, contemplation alone looks to his. Although the bride rejoices over her garden, she takes pains with it and in the sweat of her brow she feeds on her fruit; when she is led into his garden, nothing remains but delight alone. She guards her own garden but gazes upon his. Nor is she led into his garden except from her own, that is, from activity to the practice of contemplation. Or, if we admit contemplation into the garden of the bride, it resembles activity. Yes, from her many activities in due order one comes to his myrrh. Only with abundance of virtues will she enter the garden of her Beloved.

'You will enter the tomb with abundance,' says Job.* Here, of course, 'the garden' sounds better than 'the tomb'. The tomb suggests repose and some retreat from cares; the garden expresses a vision and a banquet. In the tomb we have leisure; in the garden we have pleasure. Now just as we enter the tomb only with abundance, as Job says, much more so do we enter the garden. Therefore the Bridegroom invites the bride from her garden to his garden: 'Come into my garden, sister, my bride.' Enter, my bride, enter into the contemplation of the virtues of your Beloved, enter into his delights, remember only his justice. There God, your God, will teach you in joyfulness and his right hand will escort you wonderfully.* He will feed you with the fruit of life and understanding. Myrrh and spices he has harvested for you.

Jb 5:26

Ps 44:5

6. 'I have gathered my myrrh with my spices,' he says. Immortality and incorruptibility indeed he gathered after death. Thanks to myrrh, of course, bodies of the dead are preserved unharmed. 'Myrrh,' says the Bridegroom, 'which is mine.' Truly it is his, since he was the first to receive it and is the only one to share it. For the firstfruits are Christ and then those who belong to him. Through him is the resurrection of the dead, for being the first to rise 'he dies no more'.* Good is such myrrh and better than the myrrh we use; ours prevents dead flesh from decaying, but his myrrh does not permit flesh to fail once it is restored to life. His myrrh was also his peerless and unique virginal chastity, which neither felt the first flicker nor possessed the tinder of wantonness. In him neither was such a flicker extinguished nor its tinder removed, for this was anticipated with anointings of myrrh, yes, of his own myrrh. The myrrh of others is effective and its embalming goes only so far as to preserve from corruption; but his myrrh keeps the Lord's flesh untouched by corruptibility.

Rm 6:9

The myrrh of others follows on the corruption of carnal provocation; his myrrh prevents all provocation. Theirs excludes; his precludes. In Jesus there is neither corruption nor its cause. In his Mother, though there be its cause, still there is no corruption. In all others there is both corruption and its cause. Our myrrh represses the rising movements of carnal concupiscence. Mary's myrrh knew nothing of such movements. Jesus' myrrh had neither the cause nor the beginning of being so moved. 'Of his fullness we have all received'* and myrrh from his myrrh. The myrrh of our chastity is from the gift and the imitation of himself; therefore when he harvests myrrh in us he is harvesting his own myrrh. May he find much myrrh in me to harvest!

'Myrrh with spices', means either absention from evil with aspirations for goodness, or austerity of the flesh and devotion of the heart. Whether we mean moderation in what is lawful or endurance of injuries, in myrrh the spices of both virtues are well blended. This myrrh is indeed a grace, if we are scourged when we do good or if, afflicting ourselves outwardly, we are thereby affected with inner consolation.

Abundant myrrh the Lord harvested from the field of the martyr Lawrence, whose feast we are now celebrating, and abundant spices: the myrrh of confession, the spices of confession. Delivered to the flames, he indeed confessed Christ; he gave up his body to be burned, he distributed his possessions to the poor.[7] His flesh was consumed by fire for Christ, but his heart was consumed by a greater fire in Christ. Therefore from the gridiron he is invited to the garden. Even while he was on the gridiron, he was not absent from the garden. Now he is only in the garden, yet not wholly in it. His flesh is still bound in corruption; it has not yet blossomed anew. It will blossom anew, however, when our lowly body is conformed to the glorified body of Jesus.

Then our lowly body will harvest the myrrh of immortality and the spices of manifold glory which Jesus harvested beforehand. Then assuredly Jesus will proclaim his invitation: 'Come into my garden, sister, my bride.' Then he will boast of a full harvest of myrrh with his spices. For then he will gather the result of his Passion and of his prayers, which are signified by the spices. 'Offering up prayers with a loud cry and with tears, . . . he was heard because of his reverence . . . and became the source of eternal salvation to all who obey him.'[8] 'I desire,' he says, that 'where I am, there also my servant may be.'* Where, but in his garden? We shall be in his garden, at the fulness of the general resurrection; yet even now, we are in his garden through contemplation.

Jn 12:26

7. For we enter into his garden, as it were, when with affection, respect and longing, we consider what we shall be like through him and what he has already become for us at his Resurrection and as an example for us. Why do I say at his Resurrection? Even before his Resurrection, his whole way of life displays the charm of a very beautiful garden; but what he planted beforehand, later he reaped. At our resurrection is the time of ripeness and of reaping, when each will receive the fruit of his labors. Thus his calling us into his garden, his adding that he has harvested his myrrh with his spices, encourages us to contemplate the glory of the resurrection which is to come for us through him or which has already preceded in him for us.

Is it not a joyful and truly delightful progress to enter Christ's garden, to enter the Lord's plantation, by gazing on him virtue by virtue? 'Gazing,' I say, for I dare not say approaching. For who promises himself an approach to the reality and fulness of his virtues? Pleasant indeed is this digression and surely profitable. Nowhere else is the haughtiness of the human mind better checked by humiliation, or its hunger more satisfied by contemplation, or its distaste more tempted by emulation. The comparison is humiliating; the imitation is stimulating; the consideration is delightful. The first overwhelms; the second challenges; the third nourishes. His immensity overwhelms; his righteousness challenges; his truth nourishes.*

Lam 198, n. 183.

8. A little later in the Canticle, the Beloved

himself, the Bridegroom himself invites his friends and his most beloved to eat and drink and be inebriated.* In order that a greater appetite may be born in them, he first woos them by mentioning one course from his own menu: 'I have eaten the honeycomb with my honey.' *Both are yours, good Jesus, the honey you give and the honey you are. But in this place the honey which you are yourself pours more readily into our understanding. Why do you not say 'your' honeycomb, as you say 'your' honey? Why do you now resort to this distinction? The honeycomb is also 'yours' as the honey is 'yours', although you openly claim 'your' honey and fail to proclaim 'your' honeycomb. Each of two natures is 'yours', but the divine is 'yours' and, as it were, naturally 'yours', while the human is not as it were 'naturally yours', but rather assumed and made 'natural to you' through your kindness to us.*

'I have eaten the honeycomb with my honey.' Before being conceived by the holy Virgin, the Godhead not yet incarnate existed, as it were, as Honey alone without the honeycomb. Afterwards the honey existed in the honeycomb, God in man. Now, however, the honeycomb exists in the honey, man clothed in Godhead. 'And if we have known Christ according to the flesh, now we no longer know him so', says the apostle.* As God was concealed in the flesh, so now conversely his flesh has been hidden in God. Although that flesh has been glorified, so that it is now spiritual and has nothing of infirmity, still the flesh is somehow hidden while we await and adore him instead in as much as he is God. Somehow the honeycomb of his flesh is concealed in the honey of the Godhead, while our reverence for his revealed majesty completely absorbs our wonder and our faith.

At last, then, after the glory of his Resurrection, Christ consumes the honeycomb with his honey, and without the indignity of fleshly infirmity in the substance of the flesh he assumed, he enjoys a delight divine and natural to him exclusively. 'I have eaten the honeycomb with my honey; I have drunk my wine with my milk.' Now you speak of both as 'yours', both milk and wine. Yours are the rights of each nature, the properties of each nature, without the faults of humanity; and just as he drinks new wine, so also he drinks new milk. 'With my milk,' he says, that is with the milk of your newness, not of our infirmity.

9. Run, O bride, hasten to so sweet a banquet, where the wine, where the milk belong to the Bridegroom, where the honeycomb is not empty, not void, but filled with honey. 'Honey you have found; consume what is sufficient,'* for you are not sufficient for it all. Jesus himself, however, does not consume in measure but consumes the whole, for he is sufficient for the whole. This advice is given to you: 'Do not search into majesty lest you be overwhelmed by its glory',* but he searches all things even the depths of God.* No one knows the Father but the Son and he to whom the Son wills to reveal him.* He consumes the whole, he shares a part with whom he wills and as much as he wills. He promises you, as it were, a sharing in this food, glorying that he has been refreshed.

If for your food you have been given gall, if in your thirst you have drunk vinegar, remember that Jesus suffered the like. These he tasted on the Cross but did not drink,* so suggesting the swift passage of bitterness. But he drinks wine with his milk. No longer is he distressed at the tomb for Lazarus, no longer is he sad unto death; he does not drink vinegar and gall at the point of death. The old have passed away; the new have come instead. The distress, sadness and boredom, inherited for a time from the old man in the economy of salvation, have passed into the new sweetness of milk.* Good is the wine if, when you drink of it, bygone tortures are consigned to oblivion and do not overwhelm your heart. Instead the heart is regaled with new, pure and milk-white affections in the flesh now restored to life, while at last for the future, unlike the past, no insult, no trial is either assumed or endured, either in soul or body; but the vinegar mixed with gall, which he tasted without drinking, has passed into

Pr 25:16

Ps 25:27
1 Co 2:10

Mt 11:27

Mt 27:34

Lam 198, n. 182.

the savor of wine and milk.

Do you also, O faithful soul, who enjoy the dignity of the bride, be confident that this change will be yours. He proclaims that these changes have been completed in himself precisely that you may learn to hope for the like in yourself. Indeed he wishes to banquet with you, to drink with you: 'I will not drink of this fruit of the vine,' he says, 'until I drink it anew in my kingdom'.* This kingdom he points out to you, when he calls you to the garden, to the garden of delights, the paradise of pleasure, to the ripe fruits, to the fruits already plucked by him and to be plucked by you. Then you will drink wine with milk, that you may forget bygone torture and taste the sweetness of the new resurrection, thanks to our Lord, who lives and reigns for ever and ever. Amen.

NOTES TO SERMON FORTY

1. G. speaks to *fratres* in par. 1 and 5, on the Feast of St Lawrence, probably 10 August 1166; G. addresses the bride in the second person singular, but also a reader or correspondent.
2. Compare the end of par. 1. Lam 183, n. 86.
3. Sg 2:3; G. adapts the bride's words for the Bridegroom; reading *quam* with mss Paris 9605, Troyes 419, for *quem* of Mab. and Migne; G. refers to the Church.
4. This foremost of the virginal flock, who after a fall produces fruits of repentance, would have been a contemporary of the nun of Watton. Aelred of Rievaulx relates the story, PL 195: 789-95. See Powicke, lxxxi-lxxxii and Squire, 117-8; the latter set the date at about 1160. Mikkers, 39, suggested that this sermon may have been delivered to nuns, not to monks. See L. Braceland, 'Nuns in the Audience of Gilbert of Hoyland', forthcoming article in the pages of the 1976 Kalamazoo Cistercian Studies Conference.
5. Ps 118:147, *praevenit in maturitate;* the homonym is lost in English.
6. Translating *Veni,* as imperative with G., not perfect indicative.
7. 1 Co 13:3: Lam 171, n. 8, finds liturgical texts in par. 4 and 6.
8. Heb 5:7, 9; reading *factus omnibus obtemperantibus* with mss and Migne for *omnino* of Mab.

SERMON 41

MILK, HONEY, AND WINE

The bride is invited to a banquet with milk, honey, and wine. 1. The primitive Church was happily ready for harvest. 2. The Bridegroom waits to reap all he has sown. 3. When will we be ready for his call? 4. Aelred was ready: a full sheaf, abundant myrrh, and an overflowing honeycomb. 5. We should have well-built honeycombs waiting to be filled with the honey of heavenly hope. 6. Aelred blended milk and wine which went to the heads of his hearers. 7. Aelred, once our help and now our honor, enjoys the banquet we shall all enjoy after the universal resurrection. 8. Cherish this hope of the resurrection when friends will become most dearly beloved. 9. With charity above all, we are called from fleeting joy here to inebriating joy hereafter.

I HAVE GATHERED MY MYRRH WITH MY SPICES, I HAVE EATEN THE HONEYCOMB WITH MY HONEY, I HAVE DRUNK MY WINE WITH MY MILK. EAT FRIENDS AND DRINK AND BE INEBRIATED MOST DEARLY LOVED*[1]

Sg 5:1

'I have gathered my myrrh with my spices, I have eaten the honeycomb with my honey, I have drunk my wine with my milk. Come into my garden, sister, my bride.' Take it, brethren, that this call refers to the end of the world, when with all the mysteries of the Church accomplished, she is called to the kingdom, when the Lord will send his harvesting angels* because her realms will then be white for the harvest.* Oh happy the times of the primitive Church! How fruitful then was her field, what abundant harvests it produced! What mellowness of myrrh there was in her martyrs! How many bees were building the honeycombs of a more perfect and mystic doctrine! One might think amid the very beginnings of the faith, when the seeds of the word were being sown, that it was already harvest time and that her realms were growing white, ripe for the sickle. *Why do you delay, good Jesus? Why not call the bride into your garden? Can you not already say: 'I have gathered my myrrh with my spices, I have eaten the honeycomb with my honey, I have drunk my wine with my milk'?*

Where now are the martyrs in the myrrh, where are the doctors in the honeycomb, where are the fervent spirits denoted by the wine and those innocent of evil symbolized by the sweetness of milk? Does not the field of your Church now seem stripped of such glory? Have you multiplied the nation without increasing its joy?* Many are the harvests of believers but few their spices. Autumn fruitfulness preceded in those first days of the nascent Church; now stark winter oppresses us. The years of fruitfulness preceded; now years of barrenness brood over us. After the plump and festive ears of corn, spindly and blighted ears appear.* *Why do you not cry at last, good Jesus, 'Come into my garden, sister, my bride'? Why wait? Why add delay upon delay? Is it that after this winter autumn may return?*

'They will rejoice again in your presence, as men rejoice at the harvest.'* 'Then you will bless the crown of the year with your bounty and your fields will be filled with abundance.'* 'The pastures of' what now seems our 'wilderness, will be luxuriant',* and the rage of the most recent persecution will bring to our harvests the gleaming whiteness of maturity. 'They will be multiplied' in an old age not faltering, not wasted, not barren, but 'in a ripe old age; rightly shall they be patient that they may be heralds',* patient through martyrdom, heralds through the word! In the patient you will reap myrrh; in heralds you will eat the honeycomb. Then you will toast your elect in the wine of compunction, blended with the milk of consolation. For unless the Lord had shortened those days, no flesh could survive.*   *Ps 91:15-16*

Mt 24:22

2. Even now the Lord reaps, although not as much as myrrh as then, yet much myrrh of voluntary penance. He eats the honeycomb with honey and when the sweetness of the spiritual meaning has been extracted, he makes us delight in the figures which contain it. He drinks wine with milk, because he tempers and sweetens lofty meanings and surpassing contemplations with the simplicity of faith and morals. He loves the fervor of zeal, provided milk is at hand to nourish the little ones.² When all our resources have been distributed, when the eras of the martyrs have passed away, when teachers like honeycombs containing wisdom hidden in mystery,* have completed their ministry and under pressure from the arguments of heretics have poured forth honeyed doctrine, when the babes who are nourished with milk and the fervent in spirit, inebriated with the wine of grace and forgetting what lies behind,* have completed their numbers and their days, when all this has been accomplished; 'for not one iota or one circumflex of the Law shall disappear until all is accomplished',* then the whole Church of the saints will exult at this invitation so gracious: 'Come into my garden, sister, my bride. I have gathered my myrrh with my spices, I have eaten the honeycomb with my honey, I have drunk my wine with my milk.'

1 Co 2:7

Ph 3:13

Mt 5:18. See Lam 6, n. 6; 7, nn. 16, 19.

'I have gathered, eaten, drunk'; these verbs in the past tense denote total fulfillment, as if one should say: 'It has been accomplished.'* 'Come into my garden, sister, my bride. I have gathered my myrrh with my spices.' 'Come into my garden', where no nettle springs up hard by to grieve the grace of the lilies, where sharp thorns do not pierce the blossom-

Jn 19:30

ing rose, where no tree exists to which access is forbidden. 'Come into my garden, sister, my bride. I have gathered my myrrh with my spices.'

Hear how he harvests only what is his own, only what he himself has previously sown. Truly he is a wicked and lazy servant, who by a malicious interpretation abuses his master to excuse his own laziness: 'I know that you are a hard man, plucking what you did not plant and reaping where you did not sow.'* Truly lazy is he, for in him his lord found nothing to reap, and truly wicked for by a perverse interpretation he construed as harshness the thrifty gleaning of his master, hoarding without interest what he had received and forming an insulting opinion of a good lord. The Lord Jesus reaps only what he has sown, reaps only what is his own. What an enemy sows over his wheat, he does not reap but will send angels to gather the cockle and to bundle it for burning, for they glean all scandals from his kingdom.*³ Therefore he first purges his kingdom of scandals, his field from cockle and his garden from useless plants, that he may reap and bundle only what is his own.

3. If Jesus were to arrive now, if the angel's voice were to ring out, if the last trumpet were to sound its terrifying blast, if the court were assembled, 'fire enkindled in his presence', heaven summoned from above and earth 'to separate his people',* if now all this were suddenly to catch you off guard, what opinion would you have of your merits? In your own judgement, where should you be stationed? Among his saints who will be assembled there, or among those who will be assembled in the binding of one bundle for the pit? Amid the cockle or amid the spices? Does even your own judgement of yourself perhaps waver? Who will boast that he has no cockle in his field? Happy the man in whom there is but a little and that not cultivated, not irrigated, but hiding and lurking in some supply of spices and to be uprooted from the garden as soon as one notices it.

Woe to me, O Lord, for my imperfection, if you are a hard man, if you are a harsh creditor, if you 'pluck what you did not plant and harvest where you did not sow'!* Woe to me, if you reap all you sowed, without forgiveness and regard for devotion! For not all you sowed in me has grown up. May you deign to accept the bundle of my myrrh, that it may rest between your breasts.* May the incense from my spices, barely visible, ascend to you.*

Mt 25:24

Sg 1:12
Js 4:15

But when shall I offer you a comb full of honey? When shall I offer you a constant meditation on your Law?* when a pure and full understanding of spiritual mysteries?* when the honeyed wisdom Paul mentions among the perfect? For as the honey of the honeycomb is contained in cells, so heavenly wisdom is contained in the purest mysteries of symbols, that by comparison with each other the truth symbolized may vouch for the mysteries and truth itself, extracted as it were from such cells, may attract no little grace.[4] When shall I be able to mix for you that blend of wine and milk in some mixing-bowl of my heart? This is a rare blend, that one who is carried out of his mind to God should learn to be sober,* that while acquainted with sublime truths he may sympathize with the lowly,* and while intoxicated with a purer understanding he may become a babe.*

Ps 118:77
1 Co 12:1
1 Co 2:6

2 Co 5:13

Rm 12:16
1 Th 2:7

4. How great a honeycomb, how vast and how rich, has been transferred in these days to the heavenly banquet! I mean the Lord Abbot of Rievaulx, whose passing was announced to us while we were treating of this verse. It seems to me that by his having been taken from us, our garden has been stripped and has consigned a large bundle of myrrh to God, its cultivator. No similar honeycomb is left in our apiary. In him could be seen both a honeycomb and a bundle of myrrh with good spices. Who was purer in life or more prudent in teaching than he? Who was more sickly in the flesh or more hearty in spirit than he? His speech like a honeycomb poured out honeyed knowledge.[5] Pining in the flesh, interiorly in spirit he pined still more with love of things heavenly. With his flesh all myrrh, his mind all spices, with continual burning he offered the sweet-smelling incense of unflagging love. In a body drained and withered, 'his soul was fed as with marrow and

fat'. Therefore 'with exultant lips his mouth will ever praise the Lord',* for his 'lips are a distilling honeycomb'.* For wholly changed into lips by his modest countenance and the tranquil bearing of his whole body, he betrayed the calm affections of his spirit. He was lucid in interpretation, not hasty in speech. He questioned modestly, replied more modestly, tolerating the troublesome, himself troublesome to no one. Acutely intelligent, deliberate in statement, he bore annoyance with equanimity. I remember how often when someone of his audience rudely interrupted the course of his instruction, he stopped speaking until the other had fully exhausted his breath; when the gushing torrent of untimely speech had ebbed away, he would resume his interrupted discourse with the same calmness with which he had waited, for he both spoke and kept silent as the occasion demanded.* Quick to listen, slow to speak, but not slow to anger.* How is he to be described as slow to anger? I would rather say he was not in the race!

5. Truly he was a honeycomb, because fully designed and built of clear cells, in every act, word and gesture he was thought to distill a honey of inner sweetness. Happy was he, for in him Jesus found a full honeycomb to eat, bulging not extracted. Consider the nature of a honeycomb: its head is, as it were, helmeted from the shape of the hive in which it is born. Then it hangs from the top and extends from the top. The hope of eternal salvation is a good helmet according to Paul.* From the hope of things above, the principle of all actions and the purpose of all life together should begin; they should cling to hope, aim at hope and by hope defend themselves against all temptations. If you should see a man who, thanks to his hope in things above, in every act, even in adversity, is filled with a spiritual joy sweeter than honey,* what should you consider him but a honeycomb, overflowing with honey from every cell?

If you see a man of sound common sense and orderly behavior, self-consistent in the measured control of his deeds and conduct, fully equipped with matching cells, but cells empty and drained of the liquid honey of hope stored in heaven,* does he suggest to you anything other than the aridity of a dried up honeycomb? He has a twofold disadvantage, if at the same time he is both dissipated by distraction and drained by lack of devotion. Yet it is one thing, if he keeps up appearances to counterfeit virtue, and quite another thing, if he appears as a honeycomb with cells designed in the good hope that grace may be poured in, so that he may not lack a container fashioned for the gift of spiritual sweetness and cells ideal for honey from above.

Col 1:5

6. But this honeycomb of ours which we are discussing was full to overflowing with interior liquid. It was full of cells; on either side it dripped sweetness. As a busy bee he fashioned the honeycombs of the divine word. Good are the honeycombs from which, while they remain intact, the mouths of many are daily sweetened. He did not search out some tasteless subtlety which provides matter for wrangling rather than instruction. Busy to gather a knowledge of morals, he stored it in the well-fashioned cells of his words. He was prudent in mystical discourse which he reserved for the perfect.[6] He abounded in milk-clear teaching for the salvation and consolation of little ones, yet he often slyly mixed with it the wine of a merry and sparkling diction. This is the truth. His milk was as potent as wine. His simple teaching and milk-clear exposition often swept his listener's spirit unaware into the intoxicating transport of a mind beside itself.[7] Hence one addicted to this drink could rightly say: 'I have drunk wine with milk.' Indeed he knew how to mix wine deftly in milk and to dispense either one in the other. He chose material easy to work with but you could feel in his words the passion of inebriating grace. He was endowed with a ready understanding but a passionate affection!

7. We must grieve that recourse to so great a man has been withdrawn from us; but none the less we must take pride that we have forwarded such a bundle of myrrh from our little gardens to the heavenly garden. He who here was our help, there is

our honor. And if our apiary seems deserted and our garden stripped, yet he left many sheaves from which God is well able to create bundles of increase in virtue.* God does this in the whole Church also, until through succeeding generations, when all ranks have their complement, he may say to his bride now perfect and complete: 'Come into my garden, sister, my bride. I have gathered my myrrh with my spices, I have eaten the honeycomb with my honey, I have drunk my wine with my milk. Eat friends and drink and be inebriated most dearly loved.'

Now in its most perfect realization this is hoped for at the general welcome of the Church into the joy of the Lord, which will take place after the resurrection. Yet we believe that the angelic citizens of heaven are daily invited to a banquet of thanksgiving, when any holy soul, either such as we have recalled above or one of lesser perfection and grace, is transferred into the loveliness of paradise, into gardens ever green, 'into the site of his marvellous tabernacle, even into the home of God'.*

8. Cherish these truths, brethren, remember them and pour out your souls within you. The memory of these truths is a fire; it will make your soul melt and be dissolved into delights and desires, when you pass 'to the site of the marvellous tabernacle'. 'For the outcry of the banqueter is accompanied by songs of exultation and confession.'* There both songs are melodious, the song of the friend who dines and the song of the Lord, his host. For this is the call of our host: 'Eat, friends, and drink and be inebriated, most dearly loved.' 'Friends', he says, and 'most dearly loved'. These are titles of courtship, but his courtship has no taste of flattery; it is full of dedication and love. And these titles of courtship uttered by the Lord do not fail to inebriate; they are able to woo the affections of his guests. Yet each term differs from the other and *most dearly loved* implies greater favor than *friends*. 'You are my friends,' said the Lord to the apostles, 'if you do what I command you. No longer will I call you servants but friends, because I have made known to you all that

I heard from my Father.'*   *Jn 15:14-15*

Here also notice a distinction. In both sentences the apostles are called friends, but with a difference: in one because they act, in the other because they know; in one thanks to their ministry, in the other thanks to a mystery; in one they eat, in the other they also drink. In both texts they are friends but not yet most dearly loved. Intoxication enters the drink of the most dearly loved. The very form of address cryptically implies a superabundance and means the fulness of charity. One most dearly loved is utterly full of love. One is most dearly loved who is seeped and drenched in love, whose marrow and bones and entire inner being are immersed in streams of love. One is not intoxicated because he is most dearly loved but one is most dearly loved because he is intoxicated.

In our text, what else does it mean to be inebriated but to be filled with the delight of most perfect love? Perhaps we prefer the following distinction: the most dearly loved are those who love most fully; the inebriated are those most perfectly filled with delight. 'Eat, friends, and drink and be inebriated, most dearly loved.' The friends are they who either act or hearken; the most dearly loved those who cling fast. Friends act for him and hear from him; the most dearly loved are inebriated with him. Friends are they to whom he has communicated what he heard from the Father; the most dearly loved are they into whom he has poured full knowledge of the Father himself. There to friends many things are taught, here by the most dearly loved one thing is loved. Among the most dearly loved there is no expansion of works or teaching but only diffusion and fulness of love. Friends are they who are in harmony with the divine will; the most dearly loved are they who are inebriated and immersed in the pleasure of divine love.

9. 'Eat, friends.' No longer is it said: 'The poor shall eat and have their fill',* but 'Eat, friends, and be   *Ps 21:27*
inebriated'. How are they poor who are inebriated
with the richness of the Lord's house?* How is there   *Ps 35:9*

poverty where there is plenty? 'Eat, friends, and drink and be inebriated, most dearly loved.' You are my friends and my most dearly loved: friends in the love of fellowship, most dearly loved in that of espousals. 'Be inebriated, most dearly loved.' I have brought you into the wine cellar to set charity in array within you.* Charity is set in array only when your mind is inebriated with the passion of perfect love. Charity is set in array only when it is set above all other affections. Good is the array when love holds the highest position. Surpassing love creates those most dearly loved. The most dearly loved are they in whom nothing is either devoid of charity or devoted to other business. The array is full when the passage is made from the rank of dearly loved to that of most dearly loved. The array is full when nothing can be added to the fulness of charity.

Sg 2:4

'Eat, friends, and drink and be inebriated, most dearly loved.' There all are friends and all are most dearly loved. All are given to drink and all are inebriated. However it is not so in this vale of tears, not so; but many are the friends and few the most dearly loved. Many are given to drink but not all are inebriated and those who are inebriated return again to sobriety. For the moment they are carried out of their minds but then lapse into their usual temperance. They drowse and they are roused; they slumber and after a while keep watch again. That is why the bride continues, "I sleep and my heart keeps watch'.* Yet these watches do not seem to follow sleep but to accomapny it. May the Lord Jesus grant us in watches to understand and you to hear suitable comment on her words, for he lives and reigns God for ever and ever. Amen.

Sg 5:2

NOTES ON SERMON FORTY-ONE

1. G. was preparing this text when news arrived of the death of Aelred of Rievaulx which occurred 11 January 1167. G. addresses his brethren throughout, if in par. 5, *videris* . . . *tibi,* and elsewhere, the singular be translated 'one of you'. In Aelred G. finds his model of Cistercian perfection, a *doctor mellifluus,* the title later to be conferred on Bernard of Clairvaux, and suited to Aelred, the Bernard of the North. Aptly G. takes Aelred's theme of friendship and compares friends with the most dearly beloved. See J. de Guibert, 'Amitié' in DSp 1 (1936) 500-529, esp. 518-22 on Aelred; see also the lengthy article on 'Charité' by many hands in DSp 2 (1953) 507-691, and A. LeBail, 'Aelred', in DSp 1 (1936) 225-234.
2. On par. 2 and 7, see Lam 10-11, and note 35.
3. Note the word-play: *non metit illud, sed mittet angelos.*
4. This a rare reference to one of the modes of understanding mysteries, according to a monk at *Notre Dame des Prairies,* who refers to Vatican I, Session 3, on Catholic Faith, chapter 4, On Faith and Reason: *Ac ratio quidem, fide illustrata, cum sedulo, pie, ac sobrie quaerit, aliquam, Deo dante, mysteriorum intelligentiam eamque fructuosissimam assequitur tum ex eorum, quae naturaliter cognoscit, analogia, tum e mysteriorum ipsorum nexu inter se et cum fine hominis ultimo.* (Denzinger-Baenwaert, 3016; Denzinger-Schonmetzer, ed 32 [1963] older reference 1796).
5. De Lubac, *Exégèse,* 1:602-3, and note 1: 'Enfin Gilbert de Hoyland nous indique bien comment nous devrons comprendre l'expression même de *doctor mellifluus;* c'est en prononcant l'éloge d'Aelred de Rievaulx, *le second Bernard,* au lendemain de sa mort: "Comme le rayon de miel dans les cellules de la ruche . . . " .'
6. Quoted in Charles Dumont, 'Experience in the Cistercian Discipline', CSt 10 (1975) 135-8. See also De Lubac, *Exégèse,* 1:614, n. 12.
7. Aelred's writings appear in English in CF 2, 5, and others to be published. For a fine biography in English see Aelred Squire, *Aelred of Rievaulx* (London: SPCK, 1969) with bibliography at p. 153, and for a further bibliography see Amédée Hallier, *Un Educateur Monastique, Aelred de Rievaulx,* (Paris: Gabalda, 1959) pp. 181-7, trans. by Columban Heaney, *The Monastic Theology of Aelred of Rievaulx: An Experiential Theology,* CS 2 (1969).

SERMON 42
EXCHANGING VISITS

The lover welcomes His visits and visits those who are His. 1. Spiritual love thrives and watches when animal love is anesthetized. 2. Spiritual sleep and watchfulness mean to sleep to the world and to watch in Christ. 3. Good watchmen are the doctors of the Church. 4. How inspiring and persuasive is the voice of Christ! He is the player and the instrument where all is melodious. 5. He hurries to those who heed his voice and his knock. 6. But some distort his word. 7. He praises his bride and counsels her to visit the Gentiles. 8. The ambitious should follow the example of the bride.

I SLEEP AND MY HEART WATCHES. THE VOICE OF MY BELOVED AS HE KNOCKS: 'OPEN TO ME MY SISTER, MY KIN, MY DOVE, MY SPOTLESS ONE, FOR MY HEAD IS MOIST WITH DEW AND MY LOCKS WITH DROPS OF THE NIGHT.' 'I HAVE PUT OFF MY TUNIC; HOW CAN I DON IT AGAIN? I HAVE WASHED MY FEET; HOW CAN I SOIL THEM AGAIN?' MY BELOVED THRUST HIS HAND THROUGH THE LATCH-HOLE AND AT HIS TOUCH MY HEART WAS THRILLED. I AROSE TO OPEN TO MY BELOVED[1] *Sg* 5:2-5

'I sleep and my heart watches.' What is the logical connection between yesterday's passage and the words which introduce the reply of the bride? Then there was a general invitation; now this is the answer of one person. There many are invited, here one replies. There it is said: 'Be inebriated, most dearly loved'; here she who is most dearly loved because she is the bride, replies that she is asleep: 'I sleep'. Why wonder if a reply in the singular is made to a universal invitation?[2] Many are most dearly loved but all have one heart and one soul. 'My dove', we read, 'is one'.* Love unites and love inebriates. Do you see how rightly one reply is made for all whom the powerful draught of charity pours into a common vessel?[3] Powerful surely is the virtue of love, inebriating and transforming oneself.

Would you hear how charity transforms the spirit it inebriates? 'I sleep', says the bride, as if she were to tell her Beloved: You summon me to inebriation and I am wholly free for your gift. 'I sleep and my heart watches.' I sleep and rest from other preoccupations; therefore my heart more freely keeps watch to pursue this inebriation and to drink your wine. The sequence is surprising: from inebriation to sleep and from sleep to vigils. He says 'Be inebriated' and she says 'I sleep'. A good slumber is transport of mind, a withdrawal both from sensations of the flesh and (if this also be mentioned) from the senses of the body. Then spiritual love becomes robust and vigilant, when every animal passion and feeling dozes in deep slumber. Both slumber and inebriation, each gives the appearance of withdrawal from oneself. Herein indeed they have a common interrelationship, that inebriation no less than slumber whisks the mind out of itself and dislodges the mind from its home. Each, so to speak, robs the soul itself of its pristine state and informs it with new affections. 'I sleep and my heart watches.'

Some sleep a sleep of their own and their delight reposes in their own self will and pleasure. Far from them do I sleep and my heart keeps vigil for you. After your excoriation, O Lord, others sleep, but I sleep after draining your cup.* Your excoriation is harsh enough when, disguising your concern, you leave man to his own indolence, just as your severe excoriation is a sign of your abandonment.* After God's excoriation man sleeps, for after God disguises his concern, man surrenders to a drowsy disinterest; man does not realize that the patience of God, who disguises his concern, gives birth to the rejection of the impenitent. The forbearance of One who is patient and for the moment does not strike has power over reverent minds, but the same long-suffering of the Lord which makes upright minds cautious, makes obdurate minds careless.

Ps 75:7

Is 50:2

2. 'I sleep and my heart watches.' I sleep, not excoriated but after draining the wine to which you call your most dearly loved. The drugged wine of your inebriation withdraws me from the world and delivers me to you; it makes me sleep and makes me wake; it makes me forget worldlings and not forget you. 'I sleep.' Sleep with me for you clearly state[4] in the words of Solomon: 'If two sleep together, they will keep each other warm.'* Thus gradually, in the presence of my Beloved, my heart will be more wide awake through the passion of love. My heart watches when love of you there grows more robust. 'I sleep and my heart watches.' I sleep for my friend gives rest; I watch for he grants rapture. In the sweet sleep of my repose, my anxiety to watch you becomes a more watchful dream. Sweet the sleep and sweet the dream: to know nothing else, to know you alone; to have time for you and to behold you, so far as this is granted here as if in a dream and in shadow and riddle.*

Qo 4:11

1 Co 13:12

Of good vintage is the largess of this leisure and vision. This vision has some likeness to a dream, inasmuch as it occurs not through human choice and effort, not through our investigation, but through the visit of One rising from on high.* Paul sleeps, as it were, when he dies to the world; he watches, as it were, when he lives to Christ.* May my soul, brethren, sleep his sleep and may my watches be such as his. May they be continuous and uninterrupted.

Lk 1:78

Rm 14:8; Ga 2:20; Ph 1:21

But now in a reversal I keep watch and my heart sleeps; the spirit sleeps and the flesh keeps watch; and if the flesh sleeps, still the spirit does not immediately keep watch. Repose is granted to the spirit, but the spirit is not yet absorbed and enraptured by that intoxication of glory. It is asleep to provocations but not yet aroused by invitations to inebriation, but however frequently these may be tasted, they still rouse the soul they inebriate with a vital renewal.

3. Rightly are they called watchmen, who never abandoned that inebriateng wine, who are always aglow with the bounty of eternal delight.* Of such watchmen you read in the book of Daniel.* Truly they are sentinels in whom nothing needs to be lulled to sleep but everything keeps watch for God. Truly they are sentinels whose vigils are not interrupted. They experience no feeling of the animal soul which ought to be drugged that the watches of the heart may be more alert. Some watches are filled with the disturbing anxieties of which Peter speaks: 'Be sober and watch, for your adversary the devil goes about like a roaring lion seeking whom he may devour.'*[5] Paul also says: 'Watch and stand firm in the faith.'* But not more free from anxiety are those watches in which the doctors of the Church are harassed, like the shepherds in the Gospel who watched and kept night vigils over their flock.* Such watches are disturbed by anxiety to ward off the threat of evil.

The watches of the sleeping bride involve no precaution against evil but a profusion of good. Indeed passionate love from yearning unfulfilled compels the relaxed mind to keep watch. Something like a vigil is desire for his coveted presence or delight in his presence granted. A good vigil is devotion not drowsy but alert, whether in access to the Beloved's presence or in yearning for him in his absence. Devotion is neither vigilant nor vigorous, unless the mind be restless, but asleep to the concern and desires of the world. Hence the bride says: 'I sleep and my heart watches.' And in Job one reads that 'In a vision by night, when sleep overcomes men and they slumber in their beds, then God opens their ears',* then he speaks, then he knocks. *Job 33:15-16*

4. So this verse follows: 'The voice of my Beloved as he knocks: Open to me!' Rightly she keeps vigil, not knowing at what hour her Beloved is to come. The vigils of the bride and the voice of the Beloved apparently overlap. 'My heart watches,' she says, and at once adds: 'The voice of my Beloved as he knocks: Open to me.' My heart watches and my Beloved does not sleep. His voice knocks and says: 'Open to me'. My heart watches and at once he comes flying and his voice is heard: 'The voice of my Beloved,' she says. This voice is known to me, this is pleasing to me. To other voices I am deaf, to this I am alert. As soon as it rang in my ears, I leapt for joy.* Many voices are wont to make a din and to whisper hollow flatteries, but not as the voice of my Beloved. *Lk 1:44*

Great is the prudence of the bride, brethren, and endowed with discernment of spirits, for she knows so well how to distinguish between the wiles of demons and the true wooing of her Beloved. 'The voice of my Beloved as he knocks,' she says. Whose voice has the quality to match the voice of Jesus? That of philosophers? Or of heretics? Or of the Law? Or of the Prophets? His voice is vigorous, it 'has made foolish the wisdom of this world'.* The Law and the Prophets led no one to perfection,* but the voice of Jesus comprehends a summary of the peak of perfection; his voice includes the precepts of consummate perfection;* his voice moves the affections. 'The voice of my Beloved as he knocks,' she says. For his voice knocks and penetrates as effectively as a two-edged sword.* Gently it slips in and courteously persuades as no other teaching could do. Its language is not lofty but lofty are its mysteries. Humility of conscience, harmony of morals, acceptance of obedience, purity of the flesh, contempt for the world, desire for things eternal, knowledge of the Godhead: what disputation ever delivered so much in words or what strict observance was ever so

1 Co 1:20
Heb 7:19

Si 43:29

Heb 4:12

inspiringly persuasive? Thanks to its teaching, we have learned to hope and to sigh for the grace of resurrection, impassibility in the risen body, eternity of life, and the revelation of Majesty.

'God is known in Judaea; in Israel his name is great.'* Was his name so great? Was it as well expressed? Was it so published? Was it so broadcast? 'In Israel his name is great', but not as great either in unmistakable teaching or in passionate devotion or in the countless hosts of believers. 'Of old God spoke to our fathers through the Prophets, but in these last days he has spoken to us through his Son.'* Therefore it is a vigorous voice, a voice of power, the voice of the Beloved; but it could not prevail in the ears of the Jews. The Gentiles heard and confessed and did not contradict but said: 'The voice of the Beloved as he knocks'. I recognize that both belong to the Beloved: the voice and the knock, the word and the power. With both, my Beloved is pleasing to me; with both, he charms and moves me, with his voice and with his knock and, so to put it, with canticle and with psalm.

Truly does he knock and, as it were, play the timbrel, for he inspires a harmonious symphony of word and deed. Think of Jesus as a timbrel: approach, touch, shake, replay his behavior, his deeds, his words, his life. In him all the strings of the timbrel are attuned and sonorous; when touched they ring out a sweet melody. Jesus himself is both the player and the instrument he plays. 'No one,' he says 'takes my life from me but I lay it down and I take it up again. I have power to lay it down and I have power to take it up again.'* Consider what a song he sings for you in his laying down and taking up and in his power over both; consider what is the reason for such music. Does his voice not play especially upon our heart and waken our heartstrings, that attuned like a cithera we may strive to harmonize with him who rings out such melodies?[6]

5. 'The voice of my beloved as he knocks.' Aptly does she say 'my Beloved', like one who calls and knocks from sheer love and grace. 'Open to me,

Ps 75:2

Heb 1:2

Jn 10:17-18

for my head is moist with dew and my locks with drops of night.' Charity begins to grow cold in Judaea; already the trek towards the Gentiles is being planned according to Scripture.* To Judaea the word of salvation was sent, but she rejected the word, judging herself 'unworthy of eternal life'.* I have been locked out by her; do you open to me, 'for my head is moist with dew and my locks with drops of the night'. The head of Christ is God. The Jews take pride in God the Father; they boast that they have knowledge of him. His Son they reject and blaspheme; do you open to me. 'My head is moist with dew.' Those who reject him, his head does not long for, does not thirst for, but rather ignores; therefore his head is full of dew. It is moist with dew because they are fickle in understanding, lacking in depth of reason, devoid of conviction in their claims; trivial in reason, ponderous in obstinacy, ineffectual but tenacious like dew and drops of the night. 'And my locks' are filled 'with drops of the night' which are icy and dark. For there is a dew which does not belong to the night. 'Your dew,' says Isaiah to God, 'is a dew of light'.* 'And my locks' are filled 'with drops of the night'. The Jews have clung to figures, well versed in the literal but not in the spiritual sense.[7] The Jews glory in the knowledge of the One God and in figurative observance of the Law; discoloring the mystery of the Trinity and the truth of what was prefigured, they boast of superfluous and lifeless symbols. They annoy me, they oppress my disciples, who are like an ornament and decoration of my head; so I fly from them 'Open to me!'

6. Some heretics try to extinguish the light of Christ's divinity, which they refuse to approach by faith and cannot approach by reason. With the shrewd refinements of their disputations, as incoherent and minute as dew drops, they discolor, corrupt and suppress the subtle and converging written evidence which rests on divine authority like locks of hair on the head. These also, assuming a personal knowledge of God and an acuteness in spiritual discernment, as if loftily posted[8] on the very head

Ac 13:46

Ac 13:19

Is 26:19

and locks of God, are compared to the dew and drops of the night, that you may understand that they are tiny, frosty, fluid and incoherent.

If, however, you see someone clinging to a sound faith as if to the head itself, sharing in the sacraments only for appearances and skilled in shrewd interpretation, still his faith is frigid, thanks to a bad conscience, dark in its duplicity and watery thanks to its rapid evanescence. For 'the exultation of a hypocrite lasts but a moment'.* Such a one Jesus considers an outsider, shuns as an oppressor and a burden to Himself. Such men do not so much walk as flutter upon 'marvels and wonders' beyond themselves,* in exalted pride hovering in a basket of air.⁹ In their circuitous 'profiteering, they stalk in the dark'.* They hunt for gain from religion; they pretend to possess spiritual doctrine and an eloquence as fluent as dew; they claim to know doubtful, occult and, as it were, nocturnal mysteries, to grasp the head and summit of the wisdom of God's holiness and to cling to the very crest of Christ; they show determination to reach the pinnacle but not to enter the door.

7. In his annoyance Jesus shuns them saying: 'open to me, my sister.' Since you are within and do not wander abroad, or flutter aloft, or wish so much to be conspicuous outside as to dwell inside, open to me. 'Open to me; open to me.' What do you seek but me? You are wholly mine, wholly mine, and mine on many counts. How many? Listen to how many: 'My sister, my kin, my dove, my spotless one.' 'My sister' because related in the flesh he assumed. 'My kin' because from his side while he slept on the cross, from the second Adam, the new Eve was created, that they might be no longer two but one flesh.* There is a natural kinship; here a personal union. There a sister; here a bride. 'My dove' by the grace of the Spirit; 'my spotless one' by forgiveness and discipline. In the flesh a 'sister', in the sacraments a 'bride', in the Spirit simple, 'spotless' in holiness, in all of these 'mine'.

'Open to me!' Do what you are doing; open to me! For you I am within but open to me in those whom

I still wait outside. Open, invite, and draw them 'into the site of the marvellous tabernacle'.* Knock, that to you may be opened 'a wide and inviting door', as Paul says,* that through your persuasions an entrance may open into their affections. Enter among them, that afterwards you may draw them to yourself. Go out to them that they may come in to you, for they shiver outside feeling the chill. Recoup the losses of your absence by gaining the presence of others.

Ps 41:5

1 Co 16:9

What do you say? 'I have put off my tunic; how can I don it again?' What do you say? 'I have washed my feet; how shall I soil them again'?* You have put off your tunic, the tunic of fleshly care, a tunic certainly cumbersome and perhaps soiled. You have put off your own tunic; don mine. Zeal for my house has consumed you; therefore, as Isaiah says, don the mantle of zeal.* Press on, prove, preach, beseech, in season and out of season!† To walk in this path is not to defile your feet.** If any dust clings, brush it off your feet.* Feet not defiled but fair Isaiah praises with the words: 'How fair upon the mountains are the feet of those who herald peace, proclaim good tidings.'* Do not delay, let the example of my deeds prompt you. My hand may touch you, if you hesitate at my word. 'I am a zealot';* do you also be zealous for me. Postpone your pleasant leisure; for a moment be involved in my business. Everyone enlisted in God's army must be involved in God's business when he hears the command.* Although I was rich, I became poor for all;* equal to God I emptied myself embracing the form of a slave.* For all I died, that they who live should no longer live for themselves but for me.*

Sg 5:3

Ps 68:10, Jo 2:17,
Is 59:17
†2 Tm 4:2
**Is 35:8

Mt 10:14

Is 52:7

Ex 20:5

2 Tm 2:4
2 Co 8:9
Ph 2:7

Rm 14:7-8

8. Heeding such examples in her Beloved and moved by them to emulation, the bride says: 'My Beloved thrust his hand through the latch-hole and at his touch my heart was thrilled.'* Through the narrow aperture of poverty, persecution and death, he inserted for me the examples of his deeds. These touch me; these move me. For the thrill of the heart means a stirring of the mind. Hear then the outcome of her emotion, for she continues: 'I arose to open to

Sg 5:4

Sg 5:5 my Beloved.'* Listen and understand, all you who quite precipitately and too shamelessly hasten to ecclesiastical preferment. For the bride to whom the love songs of this Canticle are sung approaches slowly and hesitantly, even after she has heard herself called sister, kin, dove, and spotless. Consider whether these qualities exist in you, and if they do, fear lest you lose them; if they do not, fear even more lest you fail to acquire them. Observe after how many invitations and eulogies she says: 'I arose to open to my Beloved.' Let it be futile for you to arise before you are summoned, for you are eating the bread and drinking the wine of that holy delight mentioned above: 'Eat, my friends, and drink and be

Sg 5:1 inebriated, most dearly loved.'* Let it be futile, nay frightening, for you to arise uninvited, when you are sleeping a sweet sleep until the Beloved says to you, 'Open to me'. Let not the voice of ambition, or avarice, or restlessness, or elation move or allure your spirit with deceptive flattery. Let those voices be unknown to you; let them not persuade you that the task is good for you, but arise only at the voice of your Beloved who lives and reigns God for ever and ever. Amen.

NOTES ON SERMON FORTY-TWO

1. G. uses an intricate alternation of singulars and plurals of address, as if the one soul and the many souls were the one bride, the one Church: in par. 1, *vides . . . videte*; in par. 2, *fratres* but in par. 3, *legis*; in par. 4, *fratres* but *puta*, etc. . . . *Vide*; in par. 8, *audi . . . audite . . . attende* and a series of singulars where the individual soul and the bride seem to be fused together.

2. Reading *invitationem* with mss and Mab. for *vitationem* of Migne.

3. Reading *in commune* with mss and Migne for *in Ecclesia* of Mab.

4. *diffinis* with mss, Mab. and Migne; see the same word in S 47:6.

5. This verse is read daily at Compline. See Morson, 154; White, 7-11.

6. See Hamlet's use of the same idea to disconcert Guildenstern who cannot play on the recorder or pipes and would play upon Hamlet. 'Will you play upon this pipe?' [the recorder]. When Guildenstern confesses that he cannot, Hamlet continues: 'Why, look you now, how unworthy a thing you make of me! You would play upon me; you would seem to know my stops; you would pluck out the heart of my mystery; you would sound me from my lowest note to the top of my compass; and there is much music, excellent voice, in this little organ; yet cannot you make it speak. 'Sblood, do you think that I am easier to be played on than a pipe? Call me what instrument you will, though you can fret me you cannot play upon me.' Shakespeare, *Hamlet*, 3:2. See John Hollander, *The Untuning of the Sky*, Princeton U. Press, 1961, pp. 206, 266, 270; he quotes Chrysostom who uses similar instruments to make the same point. See Gn 31:27, Jb 21:12.

7. De Lubac, *Exégèse*, 2:291, n. 7.

8. Reading *locati* with mss Paris 9605, Troyes 419, for *locatis* of mss Paris 8546, Bruges 49, Madrid 512, Mab. and Migne.

9. This is reminiscent of Aristophanes' *Clouds*, where Socrates is satirized as a Sophist; he appears in a basket treading the upper air, in the clouds where thinking is clearer. Vainly Socrates attempts to counter the humor of Aristophanes in his Apology: Plato, *Apology*, 18, 19.

SERMON 43
FROM ACTION TO CONTEMPLATION

Receiving his inspiration for action, the lover is led to contemplation. 1. Yesterday we saw him seek solace, today see him bring solace. 2. The bride is invited to a higher contemplation. 3. The graces and actions of God vary with the variety of attributes; his simplicity receives various titles. 4. The meaning of the head and the locks bedewed with moisture; one must guard against the deceitfulness of Satan. 5. The bride makes excuses to avoid the care of souls. 6. The anticipatory grace of God and a triple manner of contemplation. 7. The three actions of the bride, thrilled, rising, opening. 8. Regular observance is compared to dripping myrrh and to the persecutions of the Church. 9. Action precedes contemplation.

OPEN TO ME, MY SISTER, MY KIN, MY DOVE, MY PERFECT ONE, FOR MY HEAD IS MOIST WITH DEW, MY LOCKS WITH DROPS OF THE NIGHT. I HAVE SHED MY ROBE. HOW SHALL I DON IT AGAIN? I HAVE BATHED MY FEET, HOW SHALL I SOIL THEM AGAIN? MY BELOVED THRUST HIS HAND THROUGH THE LATCH-HOLE AND AT HIS TOUCH MY HEART THRILLED WITHIN ME. I AROSE TO OPEN TO MY BELOVED, BUT MY BELOVED HAD TURNED AWAY AND GONE. MY HANDS DRIPPED WITH MYRRH AND MY FINGERS WERE FILLED WITH CHOICEST MYRRH.*[1]   *Sg 5:2-6*

In the previous sermon our explanation of this passage suggested that Jesus begged for comfort from his bride against the assaults of those who try to stain the purity of our faith with the dregs of human and perfidious teaching, to drench it with the night dew of shrewd plausibility which the Prince of darkness, the Prince of the night air sprinkles covertly and imperceptibly.* Again in another passage, Jeremiah laments that waters engulfed his head.* In yesterday's talk then, the Lord Jesus was presented in flight from assaults; today let him be presented returning with joys. Yesterday he was presented as begging solace, today as bringing solace with him, yesterday full of insults, today full of graces.

Yesterday's interpretation concerns but few souls; today's concerns many more. Not all are either suitable or commissioned for the work of preaching. For not all are equipped to refute attacks on the faith or charged with this task. Not all can be mothers and brides but all can be sisters and brides. Not all can sustain the pangs of childbirth but all must sustain the grace of his embrace. In yesterday's interpretation the moisture of the night dew was disagreeable; today let it be pleasant. There Jesus speaks to register complaints, here to suggest endearments. There he hid from his foes but here he only hastens to his bride.

2. 'Open to me, my sister, my kin.' Observe the discipline of the guard here, where the door is not left without a sentry. Who will enter at will there, where Jesus does not enter without knocking and only when his voice has been heard and recognized? Happy I should be, if it can be said of my soul: this door is closed and no undisciplined feeling slips through by stealth or by chance! It opens only to the Prince, if I set a guard over my lips to open only to the Prince when he halts before them. Open to me the gateway of justice* and entering through it I shall feast with you, I shall dine in justice* and shall drink and be inebriated; in the words of the Song, I shall also inebriate you with my dewdrops.* I come not parched but moist with the dew of graces flowing

Eph 2:2; 6:12

Lm 3:54

Ps 117:19
Eph 5:9; Ph 1:11; Mt 5:6
Sg 5:1

gently. 'Open to me!' I am already inside for you now but open to me that I may enter more fully.

'Open to me!' I come at last renewed and with the dew of fresh affection. Like the dew, my eloquence will flow over you, when I shall let settle upon you the mysteries of my Godhead. 'My head is moist with dew' and contemplation of the divine nature in me begets subtle and fruitful meanings. Why do you tarry over the mysteries of my humanity only? Why do you crouch so long only at my feet? Arise, ascend to my head, open to my head. Open to me in my head, 'because my head is moist with dew'. My humanity purchases grace; my Godhead bestows grace. My humanity petitions grace, my Godhead imparts grace. My humanity pours out blood; my Godhead pours in love. 'My head is moist with dew.' My Godhead is really the dew. My Godhead seeps into the soul and waters her marrow. Up to a point I have entered, open to me, that I may reach your inmost being, that the sweet experience of my Godhead may pour in and dye every cell of your interior. Open to me that the fine dew of my Godhead may saturate and inebriate the soil of your heart.[2]

Yes, brethren, this is the real truth. Where there is greater glory in the subject matter, there is greater grace in meditation. What has more excellence, claims more reverence and confers more grace. What takes priority by the superiority of its nature, when it is grasped elicits more delight. That is more pleasant to all, which surpasses all. A special kind of vision is required for a unique object. This special vision is not within human rights, for it is not a human characteristic. This is granted to a restful and watchful mind, yet not when man wills but when God wills and says: 'Open to me!' What is it to say: 'Open to me', but with an endearing word to woo the affection and court the desire, that the mind touched in part by the flash of so much light may offer itself purified for a fuller perception? So the light, as it were, says to the eye, 'Open to me', and from a tiny glimpse of itself, light engenders a yearning for a greater participation.

3. 'Open to me, my sister.' Why do you request, good Jesus, that the door be opened? You yourself 'have the key of David'; you open and no one closes.* Your sudden appearance is an opening. Appear and no one closes to you. When the glory of your Majesty in its tiniest ray begins to flash upon the spirit, suddenly it whirls and sweeps the spirit towards itself. While your glory radiates, it allows no door to be shut upon it. The heart you penetrate, you open to yourself; you hold it open, as long as you do not withdraw yourself. And perhaps both openings are required and related, the opening of the Bridegroom and the opening of the bride. The opening of the Bridegroom is his appearance; the opening of the bride is her preparation and adaptation for such tender exchanges. 'My head is moist with dew and my locks with drops of the night.' His head is moist and therefore those who cling to his head are refreshed with its dew. Delightful is God in himself; delightful is God in his saints,* who rise from him through grace and by his design like distinct strands of hair cling to his head. Beautiful is the contemplation of God both in his essence and in the graces which proceed from him.

Indeed 'there are varieties of graces' like a distinction of locks.* For 'his invisible attributes'† seem to display some distinctions but only according to our limited capacity. For what in God is but one, becomes known as many and varied to us, as we strive to convey this or that divine attribute in distinct symbols and words. Some concern only his Magnitude; regard this as one lock of hair. Others concern his Power alone; so regard this also as one lock. Similarly what relates to his Wisdom, Goodness, Predestination, Providence, Grace, Clemency, Counsel, and in general our thoughts about God which one form of expression encompasses and which seem to belong to one attribute, interpret as one lock; those which relate to some other attribute, interpret as another lock.

'His invisible attributes', says the apostle, 'are understood when seen through his visible creation;

Rv 5:7

Ws 16:20,
Ps 67:36

*1 Co 12:4
†Rm 1:20

so also his eternal Godhead.'* Paul speaks of these attributes in the plural, of his Godhead in the singular. The Godhead then take as the head, the attributes as his locks. For the Godhead in itself is one and simple, but so far as it affects its subjects and impresses its image on them individually, the Godhead receives many titles of different meaning. Thus titles which denote God's essence can be predicted of one another, but not titles which denote God's attributes. God's essence is his knowledge, for these are convertible in reality and in each his substance is identical. Although it is true that God knows some object, still it does not follow as a consequence that he is that object. Likewise in God, Power is essentially one and the same as Will. But the attributes ascribed to each do not mutually follow each other. For these attributes, since they involve some effect related to creatures, draw from creatures a related multiplicity and therefore cannot consort together. A marvellous identity and a marvellous diversity! Each is beyond explanation; each is full of wonder; each contains most hidden and most effective motives for devotion and reverence! *Rm 1:20*

4. Approach this head, O bride, and these locks of your Beloved; comb out his 'locks moist with dew'; thence you will draw a store of sweetest perfume. His locks are full of drops of the night, hidden drops, drops refreshing with a sweetness not unknown. The time will come when such drops, pressed out more often, will produce the force of a full stream. Good is the stream which cools the yearning of fervent love. Whether you understand the head and the locks in the way explained above, or take the head to denote that unveiled knowledge of the Godhead face to face and the locks that knowledge derived through a mirror and beneath the veil of a riddle,* in each you will find abundant dew for refreshment. The reason why dew is assigned to the head without qualification, while the drops are ascribed to the locks with the added phrase 'of the night', is perhaps that 'this vision through a mirror and in riddles' has some likeness to darkness, since it *1 Co 13:12*

is less bright and less warm.

O holy soul, emulate the Bridegroom! Let your head and your locks become moist with the dew of devotion; your head with the dew of your intention, your locks with the dewdrops of your thoughts. Like drenched locks, let your thoughts be straightforward, combed out, rich, refined by the discipline of continence, drawn out by perseverance in stability, rich in exultation of spirit. Let them not be dyed in the least by the dark and cold dew of malice and wickedness, which the Prince of this night air* sprinkles imperceptibly and covertly. Beware of his deceitful dyes! Falsely he claims possession of that heavenly dew of your Bridegroom. Slam the door on him, and if he should say, 'Open to me, my sister,' disclaim any kinship with him. Any kin of his is not spotless. Perverted is his kinship, for contagion follows it. When Christ calls someone 'sister', he adds 'spotless'. Yield only when you can reply: 'The voice of my Beloved as he knocks.' The enemy acts timidly at his first approach. Like a spy who fears discovery, he taps, he does not knock. Your Beloved, wishing to be recognized, knocks loudly. 'Open to me,' he says, 'because my head is moist with dew and my locks with drops of the night', as if to say: Open to me, because I slip in, filled with the dew of grace. Open to me. Make yourself ready for so great a presence.

Eph 2:2

5. Then she replies: 'I have shed my robe. How shall I put in on? I have bathed my feet, how shall I soil them again'? You say: 'Open to me'. Behold, I have opened, I am ready, but I am loath to be disturbed again by household chores. I do not want to don my robe again, once I have shed it. How shall I don it? How? In no way! I do not agree. I cannot hear without annoyance talk of donning my robe again. I have shed a robe of wool and am clothed in finer material. I know how onerous is Martha's role, in what a burdensome robe she is clothed, how, busy with continual serving, she must keep soiled the feet of her affections and the steps of her tasks.

I cannot degenerate from a Mary to a Martha.

I have chosen the best role, to make my heart open and ready for the arrival of my Beloved. In Martha's role one does not seem to have suffered any harm; once relieved she hastens to return to Mary's role. Stripped of all worldly substance and without the deterrent of a veil, ready to contemplate the glory of the Beloved with a face unadorned and, as it were, unveiled, I will arise to open to him. This way is a beautiful way; neither can a soiled foot proceed along it, nor can a foot be soiled upon it.* Short is the way, for the Beloved stands at the door clamoring and knocking, as if chafing at delay. He knocks at the gate, he scouts the entrance and with more ardent love, despite my haste, he anticipates me. *Is 35:8*

6. 'He thrust his hand through the latch-hole and at his touch my heart thrilled within me.' What does it mean here that the bride who had closed the door of her room[3] did not also block this aperture lest anything approach her unobserved? Acting rather cautiously in everything else, why did she allow a place for negligence here? Or was she less aware perhaps of this aperture in herself? Who indeed can know all the apertures, all the entrances, all the breaches[4] in himself but the one who as we read in Ezechiel, bored holes in precious stones?* He bores holes where he wills because where he wills through the latch, through an apt entrance, he thrusts his hand, the power of hidden inspiration. 'Through the latch-hole,' she says, that is through a suitable, a hidden, a narrow entrance. The entrance is narrow enough, where Jesus thrusts only his hand, in comparison with the opening of the door which he seeks. The bride's heart would not be thrilled, she would not rise, would not open to her Beloved, unless previously he had thrust in the hidden hand of his inspiration. Hidden is the cause of the first call, concealed its reason and not yet wide open is the entrance. But the entrance is widened when the soul cooperates with the Bridegroom who predisposes, and so makes an effort, arises and opens. *Ez 28:13*

The first cause is recognized as the hand of God alone; the second as that of God and man together.

And while it belongs more to God as a gift, it is ascribed to man alone as a merit. The knowledge of God is also narrow and, as it were, conceived through a latch-hole, knowledge derived from contemplation of his works, as if it were the touch of his hand, not the sight of his face. Notice a threefold manner of contemplating: in the head, in the locks, and in the hand: in the head the divine nature; in the locks, the human form; in the hand, his handicraft. Of this last we read: 'You have delighted me Lord, in your handicraft and in the works of your hands I shall exult.'* We can also name them as follows: essence, signs, works. Signs through some likeness in their genus promote a knowledge of the divine nature which his works confirm. Signs, so to speak, illustrate and works demonstrate. This last manner of contemplation belongs to simple folk, the second to the learned, the first to those most purified. However, as we said already, the insertion of his hand through the latch-hole signifies that concealed and hidden imparting of inspiration which the touch of divine power effects.

7. Here also one can distinguish three actions of the bride. What are they? First she is thrilled, secondly she rises, thirdly she opens. The first occurs in her but not at her initiative; the two following so occur in her that they are indeed at her initiative. In the first she is anticipated, in the second she makes an effort, in the third she reaches her goal. When she is thrilled she is not active but passive; when she rises and opens she makes some effort on her own. She is thrilled, when she gently experiences the hidden movement of holy inspiration; she rises, when she consents and follows where inspiration leads; she opens, when her mind yields wholly to this work and makes itself energetic. The more she opens herself to this exercise, however, the more quickly she faints through excessive affection and passion. 'I was mindful of God,' says the Psalmist, 'and I was delighted and exercised, and my spirit fainted.'* Compare and apply memory to her heart, delight to her thrill, exercise to her rising. For the words 'my spirit

Ps 91:5

Ps 76:4

fainted' refer to what follows in our text: 'I opened the bolt of my door to my Beloved but he had turned away.' He then turns away, when you faint, unable to endure. When you are moved too passionately then he flies off more quickly. The more affectionately you receive the embraces of the Beloved and strive with an open heart wholly to absorb and consume him, so much the more quickly the fleeting presence of your Beloved fades away.

8. But now let us return to the sequence of the text. "I arose to open to my Beloved. My hands dripped with myrrh; my fingers were filled with choicest myrrh.' About to speak of opening the door, why does she first advert to her hands? Did she wish perhaps to suggest with what hands you should open to your Beloved, with what meritorious deeds you should prepare your approach to the contemplation of truth? Good indeed are hands scented with myrrh, which practice mortification of the flesh, which check its laxity, constrain its wantonness, that the entrance may be wider for enjoyment of the Word. Do you not regard as drops of myrrh these works of regular observance, which following one upon another anoint the mind and constrain the flesh? Consider our vigils, fasts, a modest and sparce diet, rough cloth and black bread, strokes of the rod freely undertaken, the chanting of psalms at daybreak[5] and silent prayer; though each prayer rises with heartfelt passion, still silent prayer is the more passionate the more a quiet breathing of the body releases the breath of the spirit. Do not all these observances distill myrrh upon us as they succeed one another? Rightly are they compared to myrrh, because they inflict on the flesh the bitterness of discomfort and soothe the spirit with the ointment of devotion.

That neither discretion is lacking in the bride nor reasonable service,* you can gather from her words: 'My fingers were filled with choicest myrrh.' Deeds are her hands; discretion her fingers. Myrrh is not only the action of the flesh but also the anointed exultation of the heart. This is choice myrrh, although there is a myrrh which is counterfeit. When

1 Co 12:10; Heb 5:14; Rm 12:1. See Lam 195, n. 164.

you see the fingers of some childish men casually dropping forbidden signs, their dexterous hands promiscuously scattering tokens of a wanton and perverse disposition, in my opinion you will not deny that they are pouring out like counterfeit[6] myrrh the bitterness of an undisciplined life. Is not such wantonness like myrrh, which both perturbs the disciplined conduct of the brethren and will beget for the offender in the future the grief of confusion and repentance?[7]

But that myrrh is the choicest which has been found praiseworthy in the many trials of regular observance. Both regular observance and enemy assaults are praiseworthy when the virtue of patience, remaining intact, is not destroyed or soured by excessive bitterness. Recall the times when the Church, still a young maiden, beat upon the ears of the Gentiles, that she might open a door and clear an entrance into their hearts for her Beloved, Christ. What countless agonies of blood and tears she endured! How many martyrdoms she suffered! With what continuous torments was she racked! Truly her 'fingers were full of the choicest myrrh', because in her travails her virtue was chastened by the trials of every form of suffering.

9. With such hands, brethren, struggle to be open to the Word, to build an entrance for the sweetness of contemplation. By the merits of good deeds you will more successfully unlatch for Christ the storeroom of your mind. Consider whether the myrrh of your toil and weariness in many trials has been found praiseworthy, as gold is tested by fire.* 'My fingers,' says the bride, 'are filled with choicest myrrh.' The nicety of discretion and the fruitfulness of anointing are meant here, for she mentions her fingers and fingers which are filled. They distill but are filled; they experience loss and gain, but not bankruptcy. Fasts alternate with repasts, labors with repose, vigils with sleep. Alternation brings refreshment, not faintness. 'My fingers are filled with choicest myrrh.'

Do you desire the delights of contemplation, to enjoy at ease the embraces of the Bridegroom, to

Ws 3:6. See Miquel 158, n. 30.

clasp him alone in the secret of your heart? Do not run to open [the door] with empty hands, with dry hands! Action precedes contemplation.⁸ The more you mortify your animal impulses with the myrrh of continence and penance, the more splendid the entrance you prepare for your Beloved. In fact the bride continues: 'I opened the bolt of my door to my Beloved.' Within the narrow passage of our sermon's ending we cannot open the door of this verse. Let us postpone its treatment for another sermon,⁹ as we seek and await grace from him 'who possesses the key of David', without which no one opens,* Jesus Christ who lives and reigns for ever and ever. Amen.

Rv 3:7

NOTES ON SERMON FORTY-THREE

1. G. writes for one individual but plurals are inserted for example in par. 2, *Et revera sic est, fratres,* and par. 9, . . . *fratres* . . . *Videte.*
2. Reading *tui* with mss and Mab. for *tuis* of Migne.
3. Reading *cubiculi* with mss Paris 9605, 8546, Madrid 512 for *cubilis* of mss Bruges 49, Troyes 419.
4. Reading *aptitudines* of mss, Mab. and Migne, though one is tempted to amend to *apertiones,* which occurs in this paragraph or to *aperturas* of Am 9:11, *aperturas murorum.*
5. *in maturinis.* See Jean-Marie Déchanet, 'La Contemplation au XIIe Siècle', in DSp 2:1950; Lam 170, n. 6; 174, n. 23; 187, n. 113.
6. Reading *improbabilem* with mss, for *reprobam* of Mab. and Migne.
7. Reading *in posterum* with mss and Migne, for *posterum* of Mab. See Robert Barakat, *Cistercian Sign Language,* CS 11 (1975). Lam 176, n. 39 and 173 n. 18.
8. Leclercq, 'Otia Monastica', 105:15.
9. *in alium differamus tractatum.*

SERMON 44
GONE FROM THE CLOISTER

The bride opens a cloistered door but finds him gone. 1. The door of our heart should be opened to God alone. 2. Three doors lead to God. 3. Frustrated longings increase the love of God. 4. The fervor and liquefaction of the soul in contemplation. 5. Climactic order is seen when the bride is thrilled, distills myrrh, and is melted. 6. Harshness towards penitents contradicts the example of the bride. 7. Melting of the heart increases humility and obedience.

I OPENED THE BOLT OF MY DOOR TO MY BELOVED. BUT HE HAD TURNED AWAY AND GONE. MY SOUL MELTED WHEN HE SPOKE*[1]   *Sg 5:6*

Today we shall discuss with you, brethren, the opening of the door. Now yesterday's sermon devoted the last paragraph of our treatise to the preparation which is, as it were, a road to the opening. Good surely is that preparation which always envisions the hope and beauty of immortality and incorruptibility, which does not sow in the flesh, lest it should reap from it corruption.* Would that I could truthfully say there   *Ga 6:8*
is always myrrh in my hands! 'If anyone,' says Jesus, 'does the will of my Father, he will know about my teaching.'* See how an act of piety gives access to   *Jn 7:17*
truth. Good certainly are acts characterized by restraint and moderation and filled with the devotion of anointing. Rightly does one open to Christ with

hands anointed, for he received his name from anointing. And perhaps he knows how to enter only through a door anointed. Hence in the temple the little doors were made of olive wood, through which a way opened into the Holy of Holies.* For oil, also a product of such wood, is the handmaid of the fluid for anointing.

1 K 6:31

'Little' were the doors called and 'narrow' the entrance of olive wood; but sleek with the oil of grace you will slip through without trouble to where understanding is subtle and mystery hidden. An entrance will open without labor, if one wishes to use a door the oil of devotion and charity. I also think Paul's testimony concerning the temple is in agreement: 'For God's temple is holy and that temple you are.'* Have doors then in your temple through which the High Priest alone may enter the inmost recess of your heart. Shut the door, fasten the bolt, except when your Beloved knocks in his desire to enter. If no door exists, the entrance will be open indiscriminately to every itinerant. If the door is shut but not bolted, it will yield and open to a slight push, for it lacks a firmer enclosure! Have both the door of vigilance and the bolt of constancy. Look out vigilantly and resist constantly. Let no forgetfulness and ignorance infiltrate; let no wickedness burst in.

1 Co 3:17

Or, if you prefer the following distinction, regard careful forethought as the door and prayer as the bolt. Secured with such a barrier, your door will not lie open to hostile attack. 'He has strengthened,' says the psalmist, 'the bars of your gates.'* Do you not seem to hear 'bolt' and 'door' in these bars and gates? Each is necessary, but against the wiles of the enemy. When you hear the voice and knock of your Beloved, when you feel the delicate touch of his hand even through the latch-hole, slip back the bolt, open the door, let all barriers fall; if possible, remove the entire intervening wall, that your Beloved may pour himself into you freely. Let anxiety over the provocations of demons be turned into security in the presence of the Bridegroom; turn your precaution for repelling the enemy into full enjoyment of your

Ps 147:13. See Lam 185, n. 95.

Beloved. The psalmist knew he had opened the door, when he said: 'My heart is ready, O God, my heart is ready.'* *Ps 107:2*

2. Why does Jesus need a door? He says in the Gospel, 'I am the door'!* Here is a surprising paradox. He is the door and he knocks at the door. He wishes to enter, but through him 'whoever enters will be saved and find pasture'.* There is a great difference between one door and another. For there is a door of one kind in the evidence of nature; there is another door in the sacraments of the Church; there is a third door in the experiences of grace. At the first door, by the guidance of natural reason, wisdom acting through its works makes itself known to us; we gain access to some share of truth; we gather some knowledge of the Godhead, not however of the distinction of Persons in the Godhead. At this door the distinction of Persons is not made nor is grace conferred. Therefore at this door one should not delay forever or knock too long.* Through the second door, by our initiation into the saving sacraments, we enter the unity of the Church and the Communion of Saints. At this second door some so stand inside as to be half outside, until they approach the third door, which we interpret as a familiar access through the affection of charity to some enjoyment and contemplation of the Beloved. This door, so secret, so intimate, does not lie open to all but is reserved for the bride alone. In Ezechiel you read of many distinct doors,* but to visit them now would require a long digression. However, it makes little difference, I suppose, whether you visit him or he visits you, except that you then seem to visit him, when you take the first step and are the first to call upon him. But he visits you, when he takes the lead, knocks at your affections, slips in unexpected, and, when you have no such visit in mind, moves you with a touch of delicacy beyond your hopes.

Jn 10:7

Jn 10:9. See Lam 8 and n. 20; 10 and note 30.

Ws 13:1-9; Rm 1:20. See Miquel, 'Experience', 151-2.

Ezk 40 & 41

3. When he knocks in this way at your door, do not delay. Arise, hasten, lest perhaps he turn away. For this happens even in our verse: 'I opened the bolt of my door to my Beloved, but he had turned away

and gone.' Why go off, good Jesus? Why turn away? Why cheat the beloved of her desire? Do you prompt her desire and withdraw her delight? Or perhaps, in this way, do you draw out her yearnings to greater keenness and warmer desire by withdrawing your presence? It is so. Obviously it is so. All the disappointments of love add more fuel to love itself, and all the deceptive wiles raise love to its peak.

Those appearances after the Lord's Resurrection, how brief they were! how sudden! how interrupted! By some he was at long last barely recognized and in a flash he was gone. By others he does not allow himself to be touched. For others he slips in through closed doors, not requiring the opening of a door. That door is indeed opened to him most of all which is closed to all other commerce. When one supposes him a captive, he spirits away his agreeable presence, come like a thief, gone like a thief. The joy of contemplation is indeed like a momentary flash. Swiftly it departs and in excellence it surpasses all the power of human capacity. Whither it goes, in our human flesh we cannot follow with matching strides. 'I said I shall become wise,' Solomon recalled, 'and wisdom withdrew further from me, much further than it was before.'*

Qo 7:24-25

Perception of Wisdom teaches better than its deprivation, how transcendent is its Majesty.[2] The more passionate it is, the more swiftly it passes. 'He had turned away and gone,' says the bride. *Did you turn to the bride, good Jesus, precisely that you might so swiftly turn away from her?* 'He had turned away and gone,' she says. What does 'he had gone' mean? He had gone beyond me, gone beyond my powers, gone through me. So he went through me, as one without strength to contain him and stand fast. A sword is the word of God;* a sword is Jesus; he passes through the soul without delay or difficulty. The soul faints, when the mind dissolving cannot sustain his passion. Fiery is this sword. Hence 'as wax melts before the face of fire',* so the soul enkindled melts before his face. 'My soul was melted,' says the bride, 'when my Beloved spoke.' You see

Eph 6:17

Ps 67:3

how he melted her soul by his flaming word.

4. 'I opened the bolt of my door to my Beloved but he had turned away and gone.' So at the epiphany of the Lord's Resurrection to the two disciples on the way to Emmaus, when their eyes were opened to recognize Jesus, at the very moment of their opening, he vanished from their eyes and, as it were, went through their hearts, as they confess: 'Were not our hearts burning within us, while he was speaking...?'[3] Their hearts were burning within them during their colloquy, but when he manifested himself, their hearts melted, losing their firmness and consistency in that passionate vision. For what else does Jesus' disappearance mean but that they were unable to stand fast in the glory of his epiphany? He turns aside to his beloved like a river of peace, but like a torrent of glory he passes through. Like a fiery torrent he makes the soul melt which he floods, refreshes, and passes through. How sweet is the hour, when the soul, melting, merges with this fiery torrent![4] How refined is the soul at that moment, how delicate, how agile! Then it has no lukewarm drop, no filings of flint, no degree of frost! The soul is a fire and a flood!

Interrelated are flood and fire. In these two elements consists the practice of contemplation. What is liquid absorbs heat more readily, and vice versa the heat absorbed makes still more fluid the liquid it finds. What I call 'hot' and 'liquid' is what may be called by other names, 'inflamed' and 'unalloyed'. Hot it is, because it loves; unalloyed and liquid it is, because it mirrors in itself some likeness of the Beloved. Hot it is, because it yearns; liquid it is, because it beholds. Hot it is, because it is inflamed; liquid, because it is informed with the image of the Beloved.

What is liquid has nothing impure, nothing sluggish; it easily discerns and easily follows. But not so much grace belongs to liquid in the absence of heat. Well is that called liquid, which not only shares the brightness from the purity of the Beloved, but also, as if heated, bubbling, and boiling over, hastens after the Beloved who has already passed through it. 'He had already turned away,' she said, 'and gone' from me; he had passed through my whole being. Swift was his passing but with no little passion in his touch. After him he left my soul melted, poured out more abundantly and striving to pass over even to the passover to my Beloved, in no way counting on the return of his presence. At the voice of exultation I was melted in a flash when he spoke. 'My soul was melted,' she says. What does 'melted' mean? She began to expand, to run, to reflect; to expand beyond herself, to run towards him, to reflect him; to expand in virtue, to run in desires, to reflect from truth; that is, she became great-hearted, graceful, and glorious!

5. From this melting, perhaps it was granted to her that her hands drip with myrrh and her mind be melted. Why do we omit the third boon which the Canticle includes? Yes, it gives the following orderly sequence: 'My heart thrills, my hands drip, my soul was melted.' Even a cursory reader of this passage can notice a climactic order; yet it is not simple and easy to assign a reason for the gradual distinction. In all three, some measure is noticeable, but greater in the second than in the first and greater in the third than in the second. For it is more to distill than to be thrilled, as it is more to melt than to distill. The presence of the Bridegroom bestows all three on the bride; that her heart is thrilled, that her hands distill, that her soul is melted. All is from the touch of his hand and the sound of his voice; all is from his touch and so to speak, from his passing through. Because he touches, she is thrilled; she distills myrrh, because he seizes her and passes through her with a passionate spirit,* 'for its voice you hear but whence it comes and whither it goes, you do not know'.* Therefore her soul was melted as he spoke.

The voice is more subtle than the hand; it moves move passionately and it passes more swiftly. A sermon of Jesus is freighted with more subtle and more sublime teaching than any illustrations of his works can produce. His teaching on the majesty of the Godhead which he circulated among his disciples, surpasses every illustration; his promise surpasses all our experience of the future glory which will be revealed to us.* If you open the door of your mind to understand and perceive it, that you may comprehend this promise of glory, it immediately turns aside and passes away; so you should also pass into the affection of a melted heart. To this voice of the Beloved say: 'Wonderful, far beyond me is your knowledge, soaring far beyond my reach!'* Yes, my soul is melted, it falls short of comprehension and thanks to your passionately violent sweetness, is unable to stand and linger in wonder. For these and similar reasons the bride says: 'My soul was melted when my Beloved spoke.' *Rm 8:18. See Miquel, 'Expérience', 153, n. 10.*

Ps 138:6

6. In your opinion—if I may introduce a digression and an added topic to exhort you—in your opinion, why does the Lord's discourse not cleave, like an icepick, the hardness of some people? Their bowels are frozen with chilling feelings of exaggerated austerity; their bowels distill no drops of mercy; they are not thrilled and moved with the slightest affection towards penitents. Why do they not feel the touch of his merciful hand? Why do they not become inflamed by colloquy with Jesus most solicitous? Why do they not hear Jesus knocking outside in the person of their penitent? I fear lest he turn aside and pass them by, that when they seek they may not find him, that when they cry he may not listen. Why are your bowels hardened towards your sons, as if they were not yours? You could perhaps have looked upon your own sons with a merciless eye and passed them by in unheeding contempt, if they were yours only and not also your Lord's. How hard you would become, if you were obliged to give alms from your own possessions, when you dole out even to your sons the Lord's possessions with so niggardly and grudging a disposition?

'He distributed liberally,' says the psalmist, 'he gave to the poor.'* Perhaps you do not know the poor. What if God should say to you: did your eyes not see my imperfect one? In your book are only the

Ps 111:9

perfect inscribed?* Was no anxiety for those on the road to perfection ever wont to detain you? He is a bad physician, who does not need the sick but perhaps gives ulcers to the healthy!⁵ If you are unwilling to seek the prodigal, at least meet him on his return. Open the gate of mercy and if you will not lift up the penitent for Christ's sake, at least lift up Christ in the penitent. Let your soul melt with the dew of mercy and be set on fire at the cry of Jesus as he calls and knocks.

The voice of the penitent, the voice of the poor, is the voice of Jesus. Therefore when you hear this voice, let your soul melt in feelings of compassion, that you also may be able to say with the bride: 'My soul was melted when my Beloved spoke.' Listen and recall his word to Mary Magdalen,* his word to the woman taken in adultery,* his word to the Samaritan woman,* his word to the Canaanite woman,† his word to Zacchaeus,** his word to Peter,†† his word to the centurion.* After so many words of pardon and mercy, whose feelings would not be softened, whose bowels would not melt? After so many passionate gusts from the south, even from the hardest breast, the frost of no matter how many years could be melted. I feel that I am drenched through in a stream of overflowing oil and that I am melting with similar affection, as often as I recall the works, the words, the precepts of your mercy. 'This word of yours burns passionately and your servant loves it dearly.'* He loves because he needs it; therefore my soul loves and melts for joy when you speak.

7. Every holy man must feel this melting. For the melting we discussed above belongs only to the perfect and is theirs, not always, but only in due season. Yet, not to withhold in fruitless silence what occurs to my mind, I shall give you briefly the rest of my thoughts about this melting. Do you not see how what is melted begins to be moved from its stiffness and immobility, how it strives to go out from and abandon itself, how from its original swollen mass, it flows downward, descends and vanishes, how easily following its guide even to lower ground or, searching

for lower ground of its own accord, it often runs ahead of the effort of its guide? In those so melted, great is the readiness and prompt the will to follow their guide.

You understand at last, I imagine, in persons thus melted a growing aptitude for obedience, the docile affectivity of a humble soul. This humility fear does not deform but the warmth of charity informs. Fear breaks the mind with violence; love softens it and, by making it pliable and liquid, fashions it at will. Humility issuing from charity suffers no uneasiness, of its own accord seeks the lowest level, and rests when it has reached the lower vallies. At last in 'melting' you have in a concise expression, the nature of a noble humility, you have the nature of obedience. Would you also like the scriptural evidence? 'The Lord opened my ear' that I might listen to him as a master.* You have heard him speak as Lord, now hear his melting affectivity as a disciple: 'I offered no resistance,' he says, 'I did not turn my back.'* You hear how he is a follower; now hear to what depths. 'I gave my back to the strikers and my cheeks to those who plucked my beard; I did not turn my face from those who reproached me and spat upon me.'* Does your Lord not step down to the rough and lowly road, not stubbornly resisting but melted and docile on hearing the fiery word?

So one who melts with the affectivity of such humility and obedience and is not frozen stiff as a swollen block of ice, in his own right gloriously adopts the words of the bride: 'My soul was melted when my Beloved spoke.' O wonderful power of the word so passionately burning! It sets the heart on fire, converts the loins, reduces the soul to nothing in its own sight in comparison with God,* makes the soul melt and run from self, so that the soul is no longer with self but as the psalmist continues: 'I am always with You'.* Therefore the soul is neither in herself nor with herself but with her God: ever attentive and as far as allowed ever following, but not always reaching her goal either to her heart's content or in that eminent way proper to a bride with

Is 50:5

Is 50:5

Is 50:6

Ps 72:21

Ps 72:23

her Bridegroom. For even here the bride continues: 'I sought him and did not find him; I called him but he gave me no answer.'* But this verse calls for discussion at leisure and must be kept for another time. What we have said will be enough to match not the magnificence of the subject but our limited power to suggest how the soul of the bride melts at the call of her Beloved, Jesus Christ, who lives and reigns for ever and ever. Amen.

Sg 5:6

NOTES ON SERMON FORTY-FOUR

1.   G. addresses one individual, except in the first sentence of par. 1, the last sentence of par. 3, the first sentence of par. 6, and in par. 7.
2.   Reading with mss, Mab. and Migne: *Perceptio ejus melius quam privatio docet quam sit transcendens ejus majestas,* although Mabillon's suggested interchange of *perceptio* and *privatio* is attractive.
3.   Lk 24:13-32, expressed in Migne, omitted by Mab.
4.   Cf. S 16:9; See M.-André Fracheboud, 'Divinisation: IV. Moyen Age. A. Auteurs Monastiques du 12ᵉ Siècle. 2. Cisterciens', DSp 3 (1957) 1407.
5.   *Malus medicus qui non est opus aegrotis, sed bene habentes fortasse exulcerans.* Mt 9:12.

SERMON 45
HER MANTLE FROM THE WATCHMEN

At the advice of the watchmen the bride dons or discards her mantle. 1. Why this alternation in the presence and the absence of the Beloved? 2. The watchmen are the holy doctors through their writings. 3. A preacher's rebuke should be taken in good part. 4. Good and prudent masters speak for our benefit. 5. Various cloaks are better removed. 6. Such a cloak is the heavy mantle of office. 7. This we should be happy to have removed by the city watchmen. 8. Some are too attached to this mantle of office.

I SOUGHT HIM BUT FOUND HIM NOT; I CALLED HIM BUT HE GAVE ME NO ANSWER. THE CITY WATCHMEN FOUND ME, THEY STRUCK ME AND WOUNDED ME. THEY TOOK AWAY MY MANTLE, THEY WHO GUARD THE RAMPARTS*[1]   Sg 5:6-8

When your Beloved has left you, he does not return to you when you will. This distress gives understanding to love and an increase of affections. Now he visits his beloved; now as her visitor vanishes, he distresses her. Alternately he ravishes the heart's desire of a lover and then restores it for love's engagement. When the Beloved has spoken, your soul melts. Your soul in melting faints, unable to endure, and your Beloved turns away. Your fainting prompts his flight. When your Beloved is present and speaks, you melt, faint and swoon; in his absence you are allowed a breathing space. In his absence he restores the forces which his presence exhausts. Intervals cool the passion of delights, for you could not endure this passion were it continuous. Why do I say 'continuous'? Does not its very beginning leave you exhausted? For as soon as the Beloved speaks your soul melts.

Later in the Canticle the Bridegroom says: 'Your eyes have put me to flight.'* How have they put your Beloved to flight except by fainting from excessive affection for him? You know no moderation; therefore your Beloved is moderate and allots for you in due time the measure of his presence. So you seek but do not find; you call but he gives no answer. Observe, brethren, the passion and the power of love. It neither suffers the absence of the Beloved nor suffices to sustain his presence. In his absence, love's longings, labor for breath; in his presence, love's longings, surfeited, suffer a relapse. O happy love, which with endless ebb and flow either melts in him or, in seeking, sighs for him. 'I sought him but found him not,' she says. 'I called him but he gave me no answer.' Elsewhere this is expressed as follows: The wicked will seek and not find me; 'they will call but I shall not answer'.* Why is the same clamor and pursuit so common to good and to wicked men? *Why, good Jesus, do you withdraw indiscriminately from both? No, not indiscriminately, but with much discernment.* Of the wicked it is said: 'They shall seek and not find.' Yet the bride does not despair of finding him but complains of not having found him. 'I sought him but found him not; I called him but he gave me no answer.'

2. O how often I have sought the Lord Jesus in meditation, invoked him in prayer! But neither did meditation grow sweet nor prayer affectionate. So I 'found him not' and he 'gave me no answer'. I found him not in person; no, nor his gifts, but sweet beyond measure are the answers he gave. O that he would answer me often when I read or pray! Yes, good Jesus, tell me 'the number of my iniquities and sins; show me my crimes and omissions'. Hide your face for a while,* that my foulness may become known

Sg 6:4

Ho 5:6, Pr 1:28

Jb 13:22-24.
See Lam 178-9,
nn. 49-52;
185, n. 95.

to me for my salvation, either in my meditation or in my reading of sacred Scriptures. Then indeed the city watchmen, the holy doctors, discover me when I find my conduct in their writings. Then they discover me when they paint my character and vices; they strike me with their lightning strokes, they wound me with thunderous denunciation.

The sacred writers like watchmen of the holy city Jerusalem, which is the Church, search out the various affections of spirits and discover the passions and the good qualities of each and the disease under which each labors; no one's thought escapes their search. As often as I read their works, I think I am discovered and caught. They pierce and wound me with the javelins of their exhortations, while they convince me that what I thought hale and hearty is bleeding to death. They remove the veil of pretence, the shroud of ignorance or forgetfulness, the cloak of false glory. They strip me of the wrappings of hypocrisy and the trappings of pride as if of a mantle. They strip me of the mantle of glory deceitfully donned, as they lay bare the weaknesses of my conscience. Profitably then, in this way I am discovered by the watchmen, although I cannot discover my Beloved at will. Like Paul, finding less reason to take pride in myself, less reason for complacency. I begin to burn with brands of love for my Beloved.[2]

3. 'Daughters of Jerusalem, . . . tell my Beloved that I languish with love.' On my own I dare not approach him; I do not claim for myself such familiarity. Jesus does not yet grant me access to himself. Therefore, daughters of Jerusalem, I approach you, I solicit your help, I put my case in your hands. I charge you with my business: 'tell my Beloved'. As if he does not know, dissembling all the while! Let the watchmen plunder, let the daughters tell, let the doctors exhort, let the daughters implore! 'Daughters of Jerusalem, . . . tell my Beloved that I languish with love.' Tell him, inform him; your oft-repeated hint will sway my Beloved. I am already unfrocked, I am already stripped of myself, I am fit now to be clothed with my Beloved. A

mind stripped and disengaged languishes with love. 'Tell my Beloved that I languish with love.'

Brethren, if a doctor's scathing rebuke seems to be aimed at you in particular, to strike your conduct expressly, to lay bare the wounds of your mind, to strip off the cloak which conceals or blinds your conscience, make that a spur for your love and not fuel for your hatred. Why does each of you construe as a personal insult what is addressed to all in common? Perhaps his discourse applies to you, yet it does not mention you by name. Let the general reproof bring you the languor of love, not the passion of complaint. And if you do not yet languish with longing for that sweet love, it is well if in the meantime you languish with shame for your fault, if you languish with repentence, if your flesh is pierced by fear of the judgement. Be converted in your grief, 'while the barb is fixed' in you.*

Ps 31:4.
Lam 193 n. 158

Confess your fault and allow the cloak of concealment, with which by dissembling you hide your acts of injustice, to be taken from you. Do not more rigidly and more stubbornly cover yourself in the cloak and wrap yourself in the shroud of hypocrisy. Jesus will not be converted to you, unless the veil of pretence and deceit has been taken from you, the veil which shame and the fear of displeasing wove for you. Shame has covered the face of your conscience; remove the veil of shame, put on the veil of confession. For even the Lord puts on confession, not his own but your confession. With this cloak he considers himself adorned; this he borrows from you. Hand him your cloak, which he receives from you with affection as a pledge of love and a sign of reconciliation. Then you will begin to languish with love, although previously you languished with feelings of repentance. Then the daughters of Jerusalem will begin to commend you to your Beloved; then heavenly spirits and spiritual souls sharing your joy will proclaim that you languish with love.

4. But from an abundance of matter concerning the state of repentance we are treating this passage, though all its features seem to breathe out something

more perfect, more in harmony with that grace which deserves to be considered in the status of a bride. 'I sought him,' she says, 'but found him not; I called him but he gave me no answer. The city watchmen found me.' She seeks him by meditation; she calls him by prayer. By listening to teachers she is found, struck, wounded and robbed of her robe. And lest anything be wanting to her crown, she is helped by the commendation of the daughters of Jerusalem, that is, of faithful souls. Observe four points here, either in her or about her: search and longing, precepts and prayers: the searches of meditation, the longings of desire, the precepts of teachers and the prayers of the faithful.[3] Are not the precepts and exhortations of teachers often received with profit by those whom both anxious search and sincere prayer could weary? Are not indolent yearnings quite often aroused by stimulating words? In Acts what is fervent is made more fervent by these encouragements.*   *Ac 18:25*

'The city watchmen found me.' Good and prudent masters adopt a vagabond style, one reminiscent of the hunter's art, and adapt their discourse to various states of mind in the hope of finding someone they may touch, stimulate, move, someone among their hearers who may take pride in saying: 'The city watchmen found me, they struck me and wounded me.' The more perfect one is, the more easily he is wounded and tender affection feels more quickly the shafts of language. O happy the spirit, which such sublime darts of exhortation reach, which they find vulnerable to their wounds, for then these darts do not glance off, deflected by the hardness or obtuseness of their audience. Such darts are not to be flung at random nor in every crowd, but only where apt minds are believed to be found, which such excellent teaching will not elude. These barbs are like lightning; they strike the heights; they shun the plain; they discover the peaks; they strike the peaks.

5. So the bride says: 'The city watchmen found me, they struck me, they wounded me, they took away my cloak.' They took away the cloak in which as a penalty Adam was wrapped when stripped of the

splendor of his former simplicity. They took away the coverlets of fantasies by which he was interiorly impeded; they took away the cloak, the veil of symbols, and introduced the truth. The simple truth, revealed and manifest, begets the fervor of love. 'Therefore, daughters of Jerusalem, tell the Beloved that I languish with love.' However sincerely anyone may think he enjoys the vision of understanding, as long as the truth, though perceived, does not please, does not ravish and inflame the affections, he endures the veil, the covering of bleary eyes, the cloak of concealment. But when this veil has been taken away, then truth dawns, it sparkles and kindles love. Then anyone enduring this passion will be able to invite others to share his rejoicing: 'Tell the Beloved that I languish with love.'

Consider Judaea. As long as truth lay hidden beneath the covering of the Law, as long as she endured the veil of blindness, languishing in fear and paralyzed in emotion, she could savor nothing sweet or be wounded by no arrow of divine love. When, however, turning to the Lord, she laid aside the veil, when this cloak was taken away from her, then she began to make her own the words of this glorious confession: 'Daughters of Jerusalem, tell the Beloved that I languish with love.' Then, glorying in the taste of a new and unwonted sweetness, she invites the daughters of Jerusalem to give thanks and by her example allures her fellow kinsmen. In our Canticle listen to their response, when they are challenged by such an invitation: 'What is your Beloved like? We shall also seek him with you.'* You see how they yearn to become sharers in her faith and teaching. Teach us 'what your Beloved is like and we shall also seek him with you'. Make us sharers in so great a grace,* that in our zest for the search we may begin to languish with the affection of love. Let these brief observations on the mystical meaning be sufficient.

6. Now let us return to what was the occasion for our digression; we were explaining the advantage of removing the cloak. The words which diverted us were: 'They took away my cloak'. Let us probe this

passage a little longer; let us explain this cloak. Indeed it is not the simple cloak in which even holy minds are wrapped. It is a 'double-wrap', that is, a cloak wrapped around twice, perhaps even three or four times.* How many kinds of cloaks have we set before you? Are not the care of souls and the anxieties of temporal administration already a cloak heavy and burdensome enough? Let me speak more plainly of my own troubles. I know what it is to be weighed down by this cloak, how arid the soil I was allotted, how barren the fig tree. Many a year has already slipped past, as I approach or rather stand by, watching for fruit on my fig tree and finding none. How often it has disappointed our hopes and baffled our labor and thwarted our expectations? With good reason do I call this cloak burdensome and the less useful it is, the more burdensome it becomes. For the burdens of office are lighter when alleviated by the abundance of the harvests.

Ba 5:2; Ps 108:29

Woe to me that the city watchmen found me, that they thought they found something in me deserving of such a burden! They struck me, wounded me, filched my cloak and after inflicting wounds departed leaving me half dead.* They filched my cloak, the cloak of simplicity, the cloak of light, the amice of gladness, the vestment of burning affection. How often was I wont to be wholly wrapped in such cloaks, to be kept warm in saffron! But now the livelong day in my mind I embrace and traffic in what Paul called dung.* The comfortable cloaks I boasted of, they took away and invested me in others that were a burden. When will these be taken from me? When shall I cast them off, if indeed I be allowed to cast them off? Happy the day on which, divested and relieved of this cloak, I shall invite you daughters of Jerusalem, with more open-hearted affection to share my joy! when you, who have experienced nothing like the burden I now lament will feel gratitude for the languor of love renewed in you! Pitiful indeed is the man who, divested of such a cloak, grows pale with grief and chagrin, instead of languishing with love! A true bride, thus divested of the duty or

Lk 10:30

Ph 3:8

the practice of solicitude, does not languish with disgust but with the quest for love. Therefore she asks others to rejoice with her and to thank her Beloved.

7. When the primitive Church sought Christ in Judaea and suffered rejection, not finding a place for him among them, not finding Jesus there, she passed to the Gentiles. Among the Gentiles she sought him, called him, and among many 'she found him not', received no response but the response of death. Yes, initially, by the princes of this world as if by the city watchmen, how the martyrs were wounded, robbed of their goods, mangled in body, divested of the mantle of their own flesh! In so many and such vast rivers and whirlpools of tortures, charity was not extinguished in them but they languished the more in an increase of love. It seems pleasant indeed, since the opportunity arises from our text, to recall the unwearying charity of the martyrs amid so many kinds of torture and death, to recall how they assuaged their bodily affliction with the interior affliction of love. For if you apply this passage to them, theirs is not a cry of lament but of glory, when they say: 'The city watchmen struck me, they took away my cloak.'

Similarly we should not take it ill, if sometimes the watchmen on the ramparts divest us of the suffocating cloak either of troublesome care or of activity that is either not good or perilous. When Elijah was being carried off he threw away his cloak;* Joseph escaped though his cloak was caught;* the bride bore it well when her cloak was taken. Elijah cast off the veil of mirror and symbol, being swept away to see face to face. Joseph fled from the trappings of the world as if from great burdens, suspecting a source of temptation. Divested of anxiety, the bride is more free to capture the favor of her Beloved.

By the imagination, as if by a veil, the intellect is prevented from contemplating the real truth. Affection smothered in the cloak of honors and dignities is prevented from hastening freely to the things of God. Worrisome care overclouds, imagination obscures and honor assails all joy in the soul. In the first there is

2 K 2:13
Gn 39:12

deep shadow, in the second temptation, in the third travail; in the first there is gloom, in the second cupidity, in the third anxious care. 'The watchmen on the ramparts took away my cloak.' Good are the watchmen; they know well from whom they should take the packsack of troubles, which soul they should relieve of burdens and set free for the tryst with the Beloved to seek and enjoy him. For frequently he slips away and can be sought only with carefree affection. Good watchmen know then whom they should spare from burdens and the straits and troubles of activity, that they may hasten more freely to meet and embrace the Word. They know whose cloak they should take away by gentle persuasion. 'I have taken off my robe', says the bride.* *Sg 5:3. Lam 20. n. 85.*

8. This indeed she said earlier but now she says: 'They took away my cloak.' She is revealed to herself in pure and naked simplicity and with her affections free for the engagements of love. 'They took away my cloak', as if to ask her, 'why, bundled up in anxieties, do you seek your Beloved? Why involve yourself in these troubles? If you do not simply relinquish your office, why do you not at least relinquish your worries for a while? We do not withdraw you from your interests, but we wish you to reduce their intensity. Do not allege necessity as a pretext for excessive effort. Why allow the good talent in you to be overwhelmed with earthly cares? Why emulate those who, appointed to office, are compared to beasts of burden? They gape open-mouthed at the earth, their maw crops the earth. With zest they ruminate upon it, they devour it with relish and though they have a lofty position they wallow in the mire.'

Do not emulate these passionate men. Be not jealous of those who commit this iniquity.* Is it not great injustice and inequity to train the mind to hit ephemeral targets but to fall short of eternal targets? What if their aim is not always ephemeral business? What if some of them, on the pretext of providing for necessities, excuse themselves from manual labor, from meditation and from zeal in the search for *Ps 36:1* truth? What if they pay more attention to business than to repose, more to frivolous talk than to the weighing of sacred Scripture, more to idleness than to work?[4] They make the rounds of the workshops and cells of the brethren, idly, inquisitively, loquaciously.

Do not emulate such busybodies, such idlers. Convert all your leisure, both what you are offered and what you manage, to the commerce of love, to meditation on wisdom,[5] to zeal in quest of your Beloved or to his embrace after his discovery. By these and similar exhortations the watchmen on the ramparts took away my cloak. These are the watchmen of whom Isaiah says: 'Upon your walls Jerusalem, I have set watchmen; all day and all night they shall not be silent.'* But let us now fall silent here; let us be silent after this sermon, to pay our debts of prayer and praise, silent for the moment vocally but in spirit ever rendering the sacrifice of praise to the Lord Jesus, the heavenly King and Bridegroom for endless ages. Amen.[6]

Is 62:6

NOTES ON SERMON FORTY-FIVE

1. G. addresses one individual except in one sentence of par. 1, *fratres*, in one sentence of par. 3, *fratres;* in par. 8, he suggests his desire to resign or to be with his Beloved eternally. Mikkers, 39, suggests that par. 6 was addressed perhaps to nuns; but G. may be apostrophizing the 'daughters of Jerusalem', as in par. 3, which is addressed to *fratres,* and whom in par. 4, he interprets as 'faithful souls', *filiarum Jerusalem, fidelium scilicet animarum.* This is not to deny that at some time this sermon had been adapted for nuns; see 'Nuns in the Audience of Gilbert of Hoyland', 11 (1976 Kalamazoo Cistercian Studies Conference).
2. Rm 2:17-20, 2 Co 10:7-12:10, Jr 9:22-23; see David M. Stanley, *Boasting in the Lord: the Phenomenon of Prayer in St. Paul,* (New York: Paulist Press, 1973) 46-49.
3. Reading *sanctorum* with mss Paris 9605, Troyes 419, Mab. and Migne, though *sociorum* is found in Paris 8546, Bruges 49, Madrid 512. Lam 184-5, 89, 95.
4. Lam 21, n. 90 and 175, nn. 27, 30, 36.
5. Lam 183, nn. 78, 80.
6. Lam 173, n. 18.

SERMON 46
LANGUISHING WITH LOVE

The bride languishes with love. 1. She relies on the prayers of others. 2. Signs of love cannot be hidden; a brother's virtues rather than his vices should be heralded. 3. A hint of one's needs is petition enough; what is the meaning of languor? 4. Passionate love brings languor of the flesh and of the mind; love is more fervent in prayer. 5. Three kinds of languor and the languor of love.

I ADJURE YOU, DAUGHTERS OF JERUSALEM, IF YOU FIND THE BELOVED, THAT YOU TELL HIM I LANGUISH WITH LOVE*[1]   Sg 5:8

The order is appropriate. After the exhortations of the teachers, the bride seems to ask from her companions the help of their prayers. Her simple request is confirmed by an adjuration: 'I adjure you, daughters of Jerusalem, if you find the Beloved, that you tell him I languish with love.' Her adjuration shows the passion of her prayer. Fretful desires cannot be content with their own merits; therefore they beg help from the prayers of others. Perfect humility always relies on the merits of others. 'I adjure you, daughters of Jerusalem,' she says, 'if you find the Beloved.' Hers is not the hypothesis of a doubter, but the thoughtfulness of a petitioner, as though she said 'if you find him' but meant 'when you find him'. I use the conditional form, not in doubt of your finding him but rather out of respect for your shyness. For you hear my request more calmly, with its indefinite condition rather than a precise time: 'When you find him'.

She is not afraid they will take her conditional request as an insult; she knows the shyness of the daughters of Jerusalem; she knows their humble spirit and that a precise definition would be more harmful to their tender modesty than a hesitant condition. 'If you find him,' she says. I say 'If you find him'; I do not say 'When you find him'. I say the one but I mean the other. This hesitation does not proceed from my affection but I suit my conduct to your feeling and to your most humble opinion of yourselves. 'If you find him', that is, 'when you find him', remember me when it is well with you. Then remember me, that you may hint, that you may carry the message to my Beloved. There is no need to delay in discussing this text. However, you might consider your own conduct, brethren.

2. Call to mind how you beg one another for the help of prayers, with what humble feelings, what earnest desires and what adjurations. Not that all of you would dare to ask us to communicate the news that you languish with love. Usually you lament in turn over the languor of one another; you do not glory over it. And if someone can glory for a moment, it is not prudent, lest perhaps your glory be brought to nothing by the intrusion of vainglory. Yet there are some who, by the witness of their life and the service of their lips, cannot hide the languor of divine love in themselves. The lips of a lover cannot fail sometimes to give birth to the desires conceived. For the spirit filling one's interior secretly draws forth a word for the consolation of others, pours out an abundance of infused grace. Even in this verse of the Canticle the bride does not speak; the Spirit speaks in her.

Aspirations in holy conferences, sighs emerging from the depths of the heart and frequent sobs, are these not emanations of the spirit and of grace conceived? Does the languor of love not betray itself by such evidence? Languor is not hidden when sobs are not concealed. Languor betrays itself when it produces such evidence. What results from witnessing these signs? Do they not possess some power to evoke wonder, so that they arouse emotions of thanksgiving in those who are witnesses? Even if nothing be said, the holiness of devout conduct amounts to a request.* Holiness wishes to be commended to God, when it betrays itself by signs. What follows? When I detect this heavenly love in someone, do I not consider myself in some way adjured to give heartfelt thanks for him. Shall I not commend in devout prayers the languor conceived, which a deep sigh betrays? I am a hard man if I do not commend with all the prayerful earnestness within my power so holy and divine a passion in my brethren, if I do not commend it by supplication and repeat and announce it to the Beloved, should the opportunity arise.*

Lam 193, n. 150

Lam 18, nn. 76, 78.

But what is any one of you doing who prefers to count the vices rather than the virtues of your brethren, their losses rather than their gains, to condemn rather than to commend? If you do not feel yourself sworn to recommend, you are no longer a daughter of Jerusalem but a daughter of Babylon. O wretched daughter of Babylon, who will repay you in kind, as you repay? for repaid you shall be!* Unlearn the ways of a daughter of Babylon. Put aside your savage ways. Cease to enumerate in the saints their losses rather than their gains. Let your malice in enumerating satisfy yourself alone. At least do not herald the numbers abroad, do not proclaim them to your companions. For companions of the Bridegroom do not lend an ear, if you disparage the bride. The Bridegroom himself is loath to hear insults to his beloved. Whomsoever you inform you inform him, 'for a jealous ear hears everything'.* It is rash to condemn the beloved to her Beloved.² He prefers that good news be reported to him about his bride and he lends an ear more readily to praise.

Ps 136:8

Ws 1:10

3. The bride knows this and so she says: 'I adjure you daughters of Jerusalem, if you find the Beloved, that you tell him I languish with love.' 'That you tell

him', she says. A report carries the weight of a request.³ Reflect on the way men usually make a request. If you report someone's plight to a compassionate person, are you not making him a request? A modest hint is an effective petition.⁴ To point out the infirmities of the distressed, the misfortune of his lot, the arrogance of his foes, to whisper this in the ear of someone in power, I say, what else is this but to prompt his assistance by a respectful prayer? In how many passages of the psalmist will you find this form of prayer! In the Gospel Mary says to Jesus: 'They have no wine.'* She does not petition her Lord or command her Son, content merely to report the lack of wine. That is the way to act with benefactors and with' persons inclined to liberality. For a favor should not be extorted by pressure, but the opportunity should be presented. Commend the bride to the Bridegroom; enumerate her endowments. Is not this to enkindle his desire, to apply the spur?

Jn 2:3. Lam 171, n. 10.

'Tell the Beloved.' To give the message is to challenge him to repay her in kind, to rekindle the embers of one languishing with love. He has a store of consolations in his heart but he waits to be prompted by our prayers.* What he does he will do more quickly if we knock, perhaps also more abundantly. This delay means travail for me but it begets a wealth of consolation. When prayers are multiplied he will pour out more plentifully your long-awaited consolations. 'Tell the Beloved I languish with love.' You tell him, you who have familiar access to the Beloved. Tell him, you daughters who have experienced how great for a lover is the power of weakness, how 'love is as strong as death', how 'jealousy is as cruel as the grave'.* 'I adjure you that you tell the Beloved I languish with love.' Tell him the news and he will listen to your cry, to give warmth to my desires. 'Tell him I languish with love.' Love does not languish but the lover languishes. Where love thrives, there languor thrives, if the object of love be absent. What is this languor but affection for the absent Beloved consuming the lover?

Lam 190, n. 135.

Sg 8:6

4. Passionate love affects at once the flesh and

the mind of its patient. It extinguishes the wantonness of the body; it restrains the happiness of the mind. It extinguishes the movements of the flesh and restrains the cheerfulness of the mind by a feeling of sadness and a longing for the absent Beloved. The flesh languishes while its movement becomes more languid and slack. The spirit languishes while it is consumed by excess of ardent desire. Languor of the flesh is either the absence or feebleness of its motion. Languor of the soul is its excessive emotion. Is not the flesh consumed by the very fact that the mind, withdrawn from love of the flesh, is turned to other things? The movement of the flesh is not felt, while the spirit, become more passionate, can hardly be endured. Sometimes indeed it cannot endure, when too ardent a love exhausts the powers of the suffering spirit. For what is the strength of the human mind that it should endure, when that heavenly love of the Bridegroom drives it impatiently. Melted in this engagement, the spirit flees from itself, unable to bear the violence of love. Similarly, when fuel has been used up and at last burns low, the flames of a fire die down. Likewise, our God is a consuming fire.* He surely feels the force of this verse, who languishes with too passionate an affection, overjoyed and distraught and consumed in meditation upon his God.*   *Dt 4:24*

Lam 183, n. 81.

O powerful and overpowering passion of charity! If charity is not tempered, it cannot be tolerated. Rightly is charity powerful, since it makes the spirit it possesses powerless over itself. Once enkindled in the mind, charity reaches from end to end mightily.*   *Ws 8:1*
It achieves its objective and prospers and grows and does not grow faint until it has made the soul faint. For just as the languor of our body is not always of equal violence but at times the body suffers more intensely, so also the affection of love, although it tends with continual desire towards the Beloved, sometimes burns with more intense yearning, especially at the hour of prayer. Then indeed the lover languishes, because a passionate spirit passes through him and does not remain. With the lapse of that hour

he can say: 'Daughters of Jerusalem, tell the Beloved that with love' I am melted and dissolve. Before this hour there is languor but at its end languor is turned to dissolution.

Therefore when you pray, do not allow your spirit to waver or to turn to other things, that touched by this happy passion your spirit may cling to it, becoming more fully imbued, penetrated and consumed. For this passion will not cease until it courses through and drains a person's whole spirit.* So Daniel, that man of desires, languished after this heavenly vision, so that no strength remained in him.* When that vehement passion has passed through, the bride returns to a more endurable and more human languor, which for her is continuous because it is not so aroused. Here, to be sure, even if she does not faint, she still grows pale with love for her absent Beloved. Good is her languor, by which the feeling of the flesh moves languidly. It is one thing if a carnal attack strongly mounted is checked by the arrival of a stronger force;* it is quite another thing, if languishing and, as it were, gasping its last, the flesh with a dying effort makes some feeble attack.

5. I still feel other irksome languors, all none the less useful: the languor of fear, the languor of weariness, the languor of sadness. Why should I not be consumed with fear and grief from awareness of a life spent worthlessly? with fear of an easy relapse in a life lived amid pitfalls? in a life passing in weariness, 'passing in a dream'?* Yes, 'every living man is nothing but vanity'.* *Would that some daughters of Jerusalem, O Lord, might tell you my languors if there be any in me worthy of your attention! For many languors in me require healing. How happy would I be, if some heavenly centurion were to say to you: 'Lord, my servant is lying paralyzed at home in terrible distress'! Please answer at once, Lord: 'I will come and heal him'! Say but the word, Lord, and I shall be healed. With a word you are present to help, since you are the Word. Great is the power of healing in the Word, both the Word which you are, O Lord, and the word*

Lam 192, n. 144.

Dn 10:8-10

Lk 11:22

Ps 38:7
Ps 38:6

which comes from you through those who are yours. The centurion felt this, for he said: 'Lord, say but the word and my servant will be healed'.*   Mt 8:6-8

But hollow is all the talk of a teacher, O Lord, if you do not speak within. Say but the word and my languor will be healed; perhaps also a languor will be begotten in me as you speak, that I also may dare to say: 'Daughters of Jerusalem, tell the Beloved I languish with love.' Both languors are good, the one passionate and aroused and the other continuous and moderate; except that the moderate is not really continuous; because if often becomes the passionate, breaking out and failing in self-control, thanks to the unrestraint of ardent desire. It does not return to itself, until it faints again. If you love for the moment and afterwards cease, that is not love. If you love and for love of the absent Beloved you do not grow pale, that is not languor. Therefore that love may be languor, let it have both qualities: continuity and consuming power. 'Tell the Beloved', says the bride, 'I languish with love.' Those suffering from illness want their illness revealed to the physician; those who suffer from love wish it revealed to the Beloved, the former to be healed but the latter to be renewed. Emulate, brethren, this better languor, which as it is created by the desire of the Beloved when he absents himself, so is renewed by delight in the Lord Jesus when he presents himself, the Bridegroom of the Church and of a holy soul, who lives and reigns for ever and ever. Amen.

NOTES ON SERMON FORTY-SIX

1.   G. writes for one individual, with plurals, *fratres,* in the last sentence of par. 1, the first of par. 2, the third of par. 3, and the last of par. 5.
2.   Reading *dilecto* with mss and Migne, for *delicto* of Mab.
3.   Reading *effectum* with mss and Migne, for *affectum* of Mab.
4.   Lam 188, n. 110. Reading *modesta suggestio* with mss Paris 9605, Bruges 49, Migne, although *modestia suggestio,* modesty is a hint, is striking, with mss Paris 8546, Madrid 512, Troyes 419 and Mab.

SERMON 47
THE BEAUTY OF THE NAZARITE

His bride teaches others the glory of the Nazarite. 1. The daughters of Jerusalem also want to know what the Beloved is like. 2. Spiritual writing, so useful as medicine and food, is rightly commissioned only of some monks. 3. How the Church is beautiful, though some members have stains. 4. How quality and equality apply to the two natures of the Beloved, so that we can say: 'like Father, like Son', and 'like Mother, like son'. 5. In Father and Son is a wonderful equality and a wonderful quality of likeness. 6. O bride, your faith and love make you beautiful. 7. Our holy conference on divine subjects is admirable. 8. The bright colors of the Nazarite and his bride have faded from their pristine beauty in our Order.

WHAT IS YOUR BELOVED LIKE, BORN OF ONE BELOVED, O LOVELIEST OF WOMEN? WHAT IS YOUR BELOVED LIKE, BORN OF ONE BELOVED, THAT YOU THUS ADJURE US?*[1]   Sg 5:9

These questions so passionate seem to be poured out with great feeling. From chats with the languishing bride, I imagine, a similar languor either newly created or awakened to greater intensity, has emerged in the daughters of Jerusalem. In a subsequent verse they even say: 'Where has your Beloved gone? We also shall seek him with you!'* As if to say: we shall seek with you   Sg 5:17

but for our benefit also, desiring to enjoy him with you. In that text they do not say: we shall seek him for you, but 'we shall seek him with you', choosing for themselves also a share in her blissful discovery.

Great is the humility in both, in the bride and in the daughters of Jerusalem. She asks to be commended to the Bridegroom; they ask to be informed about the Bridegroom. Neither uses a simple request, but she asks with an adjuration and they ask with a repetition. Now the fact that she adjures and that they repeat their question indicates no trivial request. 'What is your Beloved like,' they say, 'born of one beloved, O loveliest of women? What is your Beloved like, born of one beloved, that you thus adjure us?' To good purpose were they adjured, seeing they are so inspired. Not slight is the value of a holy conference. Through the word the languor of charity is brought to birth and the languor of infirmity is healed. The centurion knows that the power to heal is effective in the word and therefore he pleads: 'Say but the word.'*

Mt 8:8. Lam 180, n. 65.

2. Good it is if words be spoken but it is not less good if words be written. 'For the word flies off beyond recall' unless it is bound fast in script.[2] Writing makes the word both durable and visible; entrusted to the page, it will be recalled when you wish. A book is a good trustee surrendering exactly what it received; whenever you wish you may select it; wherever you wish you may read it; as long as you wish you may dally with it. Writing is a mirror for the memory because it pictures the word. There in safety you store the medicines of the word, for there they are kept unharmed. If the word has the power to heal when it is spoken, why does it not have the same power when it is read? If healing is good when you speak, why is it not good when you read?

Your objection, 'Let not my languor be healed in this way!' can be paraphrased: 'let the man who first hears it enjoy the benefit of the word; let it not reach to later or to far distant generations. Where first it is spoken, there let it be stifled; let all its value be exhausted at its first hearing; let it be interred in everlasting silence. Let it not fall again on good ground to bear fruit. Let the poor fellow who first receives this medicine, recover from his illness; after him let no one feel its curative power.'

At that pool in the Gospel, one man used to be healed after the movement of the water, but in that one man was the symbol of charity, not of singularity.* After the cure of the first man in the water, it was not said of that pool: 'empty it out, empty it out, right to the bottom; let no trace of the healing water remain'. A good movement of the water is the treatment and the rustling of the sacred page! For it is well moved when, after a prudent airing, one is advanced to spiritual understanding. It is well moved when by dispersing the words one auditor is lifted forward.

Jn 5:2-9

As the word is medicine, so also it is food. And how can you say: let the food you produce perish, let it not endure? Yet this permission to distribute food is not to be granted to all indiscriminately. The movement of the water healed only when the angel came down in his own time and moved it.* He is an angel, to be sure, whose 'lips guard knowledge' and from whose mouth knowledge of the Law is to be sought.* Therefore, and this must be admitted, great is the value in composing the word of salvation, but only when this task is entrusted to, or better, exacted of some individual. The caution then of our elders in imposing silence as a rule would seem to require no refutation; however ample their caution, it does no harm, for the permission profitably granted to some might prove the occasion of rash presumption for others, while a man might be engaged in a task not imposed on him to the neglect of the task imposed.[3]

Jn 5:2-9

Ml 2:6

3. Again, to return to the matter in hand,[4] much aroused and inspired were the daughters of Jerusalem by the conversation and adjuration of the bride. How would they not be inspired to ask about his beauty, when they see the bride languishing and almost lifeless for love of him? The languor of love detected in his bride, prompted their eagerness to seek him.[5] For seeing that the love in his bride was passionate,

they suppose that the causes and provocations of so much affection[6] are in the Bridegroom. They ask with affection what manner of beauty exists in the Bridegroom, for they cannot but assume that he is amazingly beautiful and they take the beauty of his bride as proof that the Bridegroom is most beautiful.

'What is your Beloved like, born of one beloved, O loveliest of women?' The loveliest of women is the Church, for she is the beauty of individual souls. She is most beautiful in whom all beauty exists and no blemish exists. Scripturally, as far as souls belong to the Church they are without blemish. If a blemish seems to exist in some souls, although an ugly stain spreads over some of her members for a time, the stain is not imputed to her provided it does not linger in her. Perhaps, once cleansed of the stain, her loveliness is greater than the ugliness she contacted from the sudden spread of the stain. Truly then she is 'the loveliest', possessed of all beauty and free of all ugliness.

But many faithful and spiritual souls are also most beautiful, either because by their holy way of life they allow no stain or by careful and sincere confession they at once wash any stain away.* Most beautiful in a way is one who, without surpassing all others, still does not transgress. There is, as it were, no transgression when there is a speedy recovery. Most beautiful then is the soul which dons splendor and confession,* clothed in light as in a robe.* Most beautiful is the soul which either is light itself or is clothed in light: by confession clothed in light, by its way of life existing as light itself.

4. 'What is your Beloved like, born of one Beloved, O loveliest of women? What is your Beloved like?' This repetition does not lack great affection nor does it lack a hidden meaning. But if the first question had been so phrased: 'what is your Beloved like, born as he is from a Mother beloved?' instead of 'from one Beloved', no one would doubt that the second question should be referred to his generation from his Father and the first to his generation from his Mother. For in each birth he is wonderful and

Lam 193, n. 158.

Ps 108:1
Ps 103:2; see Lam 6, n. 8.

exceedingly desirable but much more wonderful from his combination of births. Of his two natures, one he holds in common with his Father, the other with his Mother. This combination is proper to himself. What is personally his is considered to be shared with them, because he is integrally perfect from them. For he is constituted by two natures but none the less he is constituted in these two natures. He is constituted by them conjointly and he is constituted by each of them singly. From their combination and not from each taken singly is constituted the fulness of his personal prerogative, by which simultaneously he differs both from his Father and from his Mother. He differs from each of them and from anyone other than himself, not in one or other nature taken separately but in both taken together. What he is essentially by nature [human and divine] is constituted in some respect[7] by each nature taken separately and not by both natures taken together.

Simply and of himself he is God, as also is his Father; and simply and of himself he is man, as also is his Mother. He is not partially and only in some respect God, nor is he partially and only in some respect man. So in his entirety he is called God and in his entirety he is called man; his entirety means not the whole which belongs to him but the whole which he is; not as if in every part he were God and in every part man, but because he is not partially God and partially man. The fact then that he is called wholly God and wholly man, excludes rather than includes parts and posits essential simplicity in each nature, not because each nature is simple but because he simply is each of the two.

For that reason he is said to 'appear clothed in the likeness of man',* for although humanity is not connatural to divinity still humanity by being assumed in the person of Jesus, by clothing of a kind, dresses and covers his divinity. Human nature is not connatural to divine nature but we claim only that properties belonging to human nature exist naturally in the person of Jesus himself. Thus in his human nature Jesus is naturally man, true man, and truly man: true man thanks to the reality of his

Ph 2:7

human soul and of his human flesh; truly man because truly constituted by his human soul and human flesh, constituted by true human realities and truly constituted by them, not merely having true parts of humanity and truly having them but also truly existing by virtue of them. Yes, having them as natural parts and having them naturally, just as he is God by nature so also he is man by nature and does not only appear in the clothing of man. Rightly therefore, just as Jesus is spoken of as existing in the reality of his divine nature, so[8] he is believed to exist in the reality of his human nature, having both natures and having them naturally.

5. Therefore the daughters of Jerusalem, inquiring what he is like according to each of two generations, in their desire to be informed about his nature ask two separate questions: 'What is your Beloved like, born of one Beloved? What is your Beloved like?' In his divine birth, he is Beloved and born of one Beloved; in his human birth, he became one beloved and was born of her who is beloved, except that he is not so much Beloved because of his Mother as she was made beloved because of him. All that the Beloved has, he has from his Beloved Father, but not all from his beloved Mother; rather indeed all that she has she has from him. Therefore when the daughters of Jerusalem ask the first question: 'What is your Beloved like, born from one Beloved?' they do not add a similar question: What is your Beloved like, born from her who is beloved? but simply 'What is your Beloved like?' Because in the first question they express desires beyond the powers of their understanding, they withdraw an unlimited question and turn to a question more human and more modest.

We can understand this however in either of two senses, so that either the question is taken as repeated on account of the twofold nature in Jesus, or[9] that the first question because impossible to answer is replaced by a second question, as if their question 'What is your Beloved like, born of one Beloved, O loveliest of women?' were to mean: the truth of this very faith[10] which you hold concerning the generation of the Beloved from his Father makes you the loveliest among all the followers of all the sects. Your faith purifies you, gives you charm, for by your faith you vindicate your Beloved as the equal of the Beloved from whom he proceeds.

He is of the same nature as the Father from whom he proceeds. A marvellous equality and a marvellous quality! That equality has the force of identity, that quality of the force of substantiality. If there were two natures each supreme, one in the Father, another in the Son, there would indeed be equality but there would not be identity. But the divine nature does not admit another nature equal to itself. In each the equality is one in number and is a substantial quality, indeed a quality that is substance. Therefore that the Son is such as the Father is means that the Son is identically what the Father is. Like Father, like Son! And the likeness itself is each one of the two, consubstantial with each, and it is one and the same substance with each one of the two. The substance not only confers subsistence but is itself subsistent, living, powerful and intelligent.

6. Such a one you proclaim your Beloved, born of a Father Beloved; such a one you define him. If it is possible, explain to us the reason for this faith and it is enough for us. 'Show us the Father, and it is enough for us.'* How shall we know what your Beloved is like, born from a Father Beloved, if you do not teach us what the Father is like from whom he proceeds? But this explanation belongs neither to the present time nor to our present capacity; it is enough however, to believe that the Son is such as the Father is. Although we are incapable of grasping what that likeness is, teach us what is his likeness according to our humanity in which he is the Beloved born of a Mother beloved.

Jo 14:8

Teach and tell 'what your Beloved is like'. It delights us to hear again what we have already heard about him. Repeat for us what either must be believed or can be grasped about your Beloved. To hear both fills us with passionate delight, and what exceeds our capacity, captivates us none the less; we have been captivated with your own fervor of wonder and love, because we see you so captivated, so arrested, so inflamed. O what is he like? O how lovable is your Beloved? For love of him ever increases in you, because to you he is ever the Beloved born of the Beloved, indeed ever more Beloved born of the most Beloved. Your love of him makes you beautiful; your encounter with him makes you desirous and your desire for him makes you fretful. For it is thanks to your fretful and yearning affection that you so adjure us. 'What is your Beloved like, born from one Beloved, that you so adjure us?' How beautiful is he, for he does not tolerate the existence of anything ugly in you and therefore made you the most beautiful of women! How lovable and gracious is he, for you cannot bear to be without him even for an instant and for his sake you so adjure us!

7. I ask you, daughters of Jerusalem, daughters of this earthly Jerusalem, why you do not address these repeated questions to the Church? Why do you pretend not to learn of these two births in Christ, in whom you refuse to believe? Why do you not consider yourselves adjured by the Church, when evidence is brought before you based on faith in your own Scriptures, on spiritual graces bestowed upon the same faith, on martyrdom suffered for the same faith? Why do you not consider yourselves, as it were, adjured by the Church in the more appropriate ceremonies she observes, in the more subtle tenets she expounds, in the higher rewards she expects, in the stricter vows by which she forms herself? Stricter discipline, more integrated doctrine, a more simple liturgy, and more eminent virtue could beget zeal in each of you, challenge your affection and possess the power of adjuration to arouse your emulation.

But a time will come, for it is not yet, when after your conversion to the Lord the veil of ignorance and pretence will be taken away. Then restored to your senses, as it were, and receiving the Spirit of the Lord, you will understand the power of these adjurations;

then awakened to a holy curiosity you will eagerly repeat these questions, asking: 'What is your Beloved like, born of one Beloved, O loveliest of women? What is your Beloved like, that you have so adjured us?' The hour of the Jews has not yet come, my brethren, but ours is ever at hand. Therefore omitting frivolous and deceitful talk, let us engage in the interchange of such questions and expressions of wonder in our communities.[11]

8. May you be the kind of daughters who long to hear such truths! May I also be the kind of bride from whom you may have the strength and readiness to seek such truths! O truly blissful mother who deserves to hear this apostrophe addressed to herself, 'Loveliest of women'. Blissful assuredly if she keeps so much beauty unsullied. 'Her Nazarites were purer than snow,' says Jeremiah, 'whiter than milk, more ruddy than coral, more beautiful than sapphire. Now their countenance is blacker than soot.'* Great certainty is this commendation but pitiful is this transformation! Purity of snow, whiteness of milk, red glow of coral, brightness and beauty of sapphire are overlaid with the blackness of soot. 'Now their countenance is blacker than soot; they are not recognized in the squares.'* Indeed they are no longer recognized as Nazarites in the squares.

Lm 4:7-8

Lm 4:8

I shall be silent about others. Behold the men of our Order! How admired their name used to be over the face of the earth!* In the beginning when they were rarely seen in the squares they were at once recognized for the sign of holiness in them. But now they are distinguished and marked out from others by little or no difference in religious observance, by little or no distinction in their way of life. Therefore they are not recognized as Nazarites in the squares. To haunt the squares tarnishes the Nazarites' color and gives them a foreign look. 'Their excellent color has changed; the stones of the sanctuary have been scattered at the head of all the squares.'* Therefore 'they are not recognized in the squares'. Not recognized in them is their purity of birth, nor whiteness, nor ruddiness, nor beauty. For whatever these colors

Ps 8:2

Lm 4:1. Lam 195, n. 162.

signify, they portray great beauty. Therefore 'they are not recognized in the streets'.

These are the colors of Nazarites; these are the colors of the bride and of the Bridegroom. For the bride also speaks in this passage and says: 'My Beloved is radiant and ruddy.' Such is our Nazarite to whom the colors of Nazarites are compared and also the colors of the bride. For she is a Nazarite, vowing and espousing herself to the Nazarite, Lord Jesus. Now when we discover her as a Nazarite, let us commend her beauty and consult her experience.[12] 'What is your Beloved like, born of one Beloved, O loveliest of women? What is your Beloved like, that you have so adjured us?' But at last let her compose the praises of her Beloved, the Lord Jesus who lives and reigns for ever and ever. Amen.

NOTES ON SERMON FORTY-SEVEN

1. G. addresses one individual throughout, except *dicitis* in par. 2, *fratres mei*, in par. 7, and throughout par. 8.
2. Horace, Ep. 1:18:71; see also his *Ars Poetica*, 390; see Lam 178, n. 48.
3. RB 38:5. See Bouton, *Fiches Cisterciennes*, 150-51; J. M. Canivez, *Statuta Capitulorum Generalium Ordinis Cisterciensis* (Louvain: 1933-39) I:26 (Mikkers).
4. Reading *revertamur* of mss and Migne, for *revertamus* of Mab.
5. On *curiositas,* and *sancta curiositas* below, par. 7, see Lam 184, n. 92.
6. Reading *affectus* of mss and Migne for *effectus* of Mab.
7. *naturalis ejus essentialitas secundum quid.*
8. Reading *sic* for *sed* with mss; Paris 9605 omits the line; Madrid 512, for *divinae* reads *dominicae* and concludes: *utrobique naturalia habens et naturaliter.*
9. Reading: *Possumus autem utroque sensu haec* (mss Paris 9605, 8564, 473, 474, Bruges 49, Madrid 512, but *hoc* in Mab. and Migne) *intelligere, ut aut interrogatio propter geminam in Iesu naturam* accipiatur congeminata, aut (mss Paris 9604, 8546, 473, 474, Bruges 49, Madrid 512; for *dum* of ms Troyes 419, *cur* of Mab. and Migne) *illa prior quasi incapabilis hac sequenti sit revocata: Qualis est dilectus tuus,* etc.
10. Reading *hujusce* for *Hujus te* and linking this with the preceding sentence, despite the mss, Mab. and Migne.
11. Lam 175, n. 34, and 18, n. 75.
12. Miquel 152, n. 5.

SERMON 48
RADIANT WITH LIGHT, RED WITH FIRE

The bride shows her Beloved radiant with light and red with fire. 1. His bride teaches her daughters about the Bridegroom; 2-3. that they also may be transparent with truth and aflame with love.

RADIANT AND RUDDY IS MY BELOVED DISTINGUISHED AMONG TEN THOUSAND*[1]   *Sg 5:10*

'Radiant and ruddy is my Beloved, distinguished among ten thousand.' The bride interrupts her quest for her Beloved for a time, but only a brief time, to instruct her daughters. She interrupts what is delightful for what is necessary, but not without love does she review in memory her eulogy of her Bridegroom. Sweet indeed to the lips of the bride are her praises of the Bridegroom. As a loving mother and a prudent bride she instructs her daughters and commends her Beloved. Rightly is she prudent, having topics so well prepared and abundant to discuss about the Bridegroom. Lovingly everything about him she has noted and pondered and it is on the tip of her tongue. Every detail elicits her affection for it is so firmly fixed in her memory. His color, head, hair, eyes, cheeks, lips, hands, body, legs, feet, throat, all these are described figuratively in her praise of the Bridegroom. And as if summarizing the whole description in a phrase and a brief heading she says: 'He is wholly desirable.' Then in order to show that in these words the nourishment of her love is prepared, she says: 'Such is my Beloved and he is my friend.'

In all this observe the teaching of the bride, observe her devotion, observe her loving preparation, whether seeking her Beloved or instructing her daughters or recalling his praises. She adjures earnestly, she answers readily, she illustrates with ornaments, she divides distinctly, she reviews briefly, she sums up concisely and I do not know whether she expresses sufficiently. I know indeed that she concludes affectionately: 'Such is my Beloved and he is my friend.' Great is the compass of these praises and obviously great is her love when she praises.

2. Let us now review the individual details of this praise. 'Radiant and ruddy is my Beloved, distinguished among ten thousand.' This is a singular blend of colors, which only in the person of the Lord Jesus converged into one by the action of God, not so as to be a unity but to be in unity. O gracious and surpassingly lovable Bridegroom in whom the divine generation is radiant and the human generation is ruddy! For he is the radiance of eternal light;* even if 'not born of blood nor of the will of the flesh nor of man's will',* yet he is born of the blood of a Mother. But there is in him nothing of that scarlet of which Isaiah speaks: 'If your sins were as red as scarlet, they shall become like bleached wool.'*

The whiteness of wool and the blush of scarlet do not blend together, do not tolerate each other. There is indeed another redness which is found together with radiance in the apparel of Jesus. 'Why,' says Isaiah, 'is your apparel red?'* The apparel of the Lord Jesus, his nature from virginal birth, radiant with the purity and innocence of holiness, in the affections of believers glows with a more comely red from the color of his Passion freely embraced. What is the quality of this red which lacks no longing to cleanse all things? 'They have washed their robes,' we read, 'and have bleached them in the blood of the Lamb.'*

3. This red in my Jesus discovers but did not create this radiance; but his red makes, because it

Ws 7:26

Jn 1:12

Is 1:18

Is 63:2

Rv 7:14

does not discover, radiance in us. His red, drawn over the color of our blood-stained birth and our personal sins, changes our red into his radiance, by faith cleansing our hearts. Yes we have been justified by faith in the blood of Jesus.* Well does his blood poured out for you glow red for you, if it kindles in your spirit the desire to make some return. Well does his blood glow red for you, if the exceeding love of God gleams like red gold for you in the blood shed for you. Yes, Jesus so loved his bride that he washed her in his blood. Love is a red flame; it makes the Lord Jesus blood-red for me. In him truth is radiant for me and love is blood-red. *Rm 5:1, 9*

'My Beloved,' says the bride, 'is radiant and blood-red.' Should he not be radiant? 'God is indeed the light and in him is no darkness.'* Should he not be blood-red? God is indeed the fire and came to cast fire upon earth.* If he offers you the light of understanding, for you he is radiant; but if he does not inflame your spirit to love, you do not experience him as blood-red. In himself he is both light and fire, but for you he is not light and fire except when you experience the effect of both. If you are a bride emulate the blending of this twofold color from your Bridegroom, that you may be alike radiant and blood-red, that is transparent and aflame. For as he possesses the power to clarify so also he has the power to set aflame. One who approaches him, approaches fire.* *1 Jo 1:5* *Lk 12:49* *Heb 1:29*

'This is the end of Abbot Gilbert's ***Sermones in Cantica***. Overtaken by death like Bernard, he could not complete them', Mab. He could not say: ***Finis coronat opus***; that was left for John of Ford.[2] This incomplete sermon may have inspired 'The Burning Babe', a poem by the Elizabethan martyr, St Robert Southwell (1561–1595). Though allowed no writing materials in prison, Robert was allowed three favorite volumes, his breviary, a bible and his volume of St Bernard which he especially requested 'for his solace'; the volume may well have included Gilbert's 'sermons on the Canticle'.[3]

NOTES ON SERMON FORTY-EIGHT

1. G. continues his instruction for one individual, though notice *videte* in par. 1. In the last sermons he shows no loss of vigor, no intention to discontinue. His abrupt ending is a surprise and suggests his realization that another would continue his work as he continued Bernard's work, the loving work of the Bridegroom.

2. John of Ford, *Sermons on the Final Verses of the Song of Songs*, translated by Wendy Mary Beckett, Volume I (CF 29: Kalamazoo, 1977), others forthcoming. The critical edition by Edmund Mikkers and Hilary Costello appears in *Corpus Christianorum Continuatio Mediaevalis*, XVII & XVIII.

3. See Pierre Janelle, *Robert Southwell the Writer* (London: Sheed and Ward, 1935) p. 68 and n. 35.

Gilbert of Hoyland

MIRA SIMPLICITAS

An unpublished earlier version of Sermons One and Two.

§

ABBREVIATIONS

The following abbreviations are used in the marginal notes of the edition:

B   the MS Bodley 24, used with permission of the Keeper of Western MSS, the Bodleian Library, Oxford.
BRa   where MSS Bodley 24 and Rawlinson G. 38 agree.
M   Migne, *Patres Latini*, vol. 184, edition of 1854.
Ra   the MS Rawlinson G. 38, used with permission of the Keeper of Western MSS, the Bodleian Library, Oxford. (Ra continues in the same hand with a work of Abbot Serlo of Savigny, on the Lord's prayer, beginning: *Servis Christi conservus eorum*, and ending: *dulcedo cordium, Jesus Christus, qui est Deus benedictus in saecula. Amen.*)
S   Gilbert's *Sermones* with number and paragraph in Migne.
Vulg.   reading of the Vulgate, *Biblia Sacra*, Rome: Desclée, 1927.

MIRA SIMPLICITAS

Cant 3:1

IN LECTULO MEO, PER NOCTES, QUAESIVI QUEM DILIGIT ANIMA MEA; QUAESIVI ILLUM ET NON INVENI*

1. Mira simplicitas sonat in verbis, piis suavitas auribus, et nescio, immo plane scio, quia mirabiliora sunt sacramenta quae latent. Reddunt me et mysteria stupidum et verba affectum et amatorio penitus afflatum blandimento. O quanta dulcedo in nucleo, si tanta redundat in cortice! Mysteria latent et cum labore eruuntur; verborum autem dulcedo in promptu est et ultro se offert, animis sine difficultate puris illapsa. Nos ergo non ita intendimus mysteriis, ut discedamus a modulis, cantica enim sunt et cantari malunt quam disputari, et nescio si evidentius possint edisseri quam cum cantantur. Favi enim sunt, et dum edisseruntur, cernuntur, dum cantantur, gustantur. Longe vero differenter respondet favi sapor palato, species oculo. Habent haec cantica laetis inmixta lugubria et gaudiis intextos gemitus, pro vario canentis affectu, sicut illa dilecto vel ex voto fruitur

S 1:1, M 11A

vel praeter votum fraudatur.*[1]

2. Et nunc quod in manibus est, querulum quiddam sonare videtur et sponsi absentis causari

A WONDERFUL SIMPLICITY

IN MY LITTLE BED BY NIGHT I SOUGHT HIM WHOM MY SOUL LOVES. I SOUGHT HIM AND DID NOT FIND HIM.*   *Sg 3:1*

1. A wonderful simplicity rings out in these words, charming to pious ears, and I know not whether, or rather I know full well that the mysteries hidden beneath the words are more wonderful.[1] I am thunderstruck by the mysteries, full of affection at the words, deeply inspired by the wooing of love. O how much sweetness exists in the kernel, if so much is tasted in the shell.[2] Mysteries lie hidden to be dug out with effort, but the charm of the words is on the surface, offered gratuitously, slipping without effort into pure souls. Now we do not so much pay attention to the mysteries, as to disregard the melody, for these are songs and prefer to be sung rather than debated, and I know not whether they can be analyzed more clearly than when they are sung. Indeed they are honeycombs: when they are analyzed they are seen by the eye, but when they are sung they are savored by the tongue. In very different ways does the taste of the honeycomb tickle the palate and the sight of the honeycomb greet the eye. These songs blend sorrow and joy, weave grief with happiness, to correspond with the changing affections of the singer, as now according to her wish she enjoys her Beloved or again contrary to her wish she is deprived of his presence.

2. Now in the verse we are discussing, the bride seems to sing a plaintive song and to chide her Spouse

latebras, sic enim ait: 'in lectulo meo per noctes quaesivi quem diligit anima mea; quaesivi illum et non inveni'.* Dulce satis est te, bone Jesu, quaerere, dulcius tenere; in uno pius labor, plena in altero laetitia.* Si enim obvenit salus mulieri illi, felici furto tangenti fimbriam,* quid erit tenenti et amplexanti substantiam? Turba et premebat,* sed illa sola tangebat, forte quia turba se turbulenter ingessit, illa sobrie et silenter accessit. Illa te necdum a facie sed a posteriore tetigit,* et fluxus in ea sanguinis stetit. Stetit enim in ea omnis fluxus carnalis illecebrae, carnalis delectationis et curae, et restricta sunt et desiccata sunt, quae prius in ea fluxa et dissoluta et lascivientia erant, et totum hoc ad tactum fimbriae vestimenti tui. Plena benedictione huius* fimbria, descendit enim et defluxit unguentum de capite in oram vestimenti.* Ideo myrrha et gutta a vestimentis tuis;* myrrha quidem a vestimentis, sed myrrha prima a labiis, labia enim tua, lilia distillantia myrrham primam.* Quod si tanta in contactu fimbriae gratia, quid si caput ipsum amplexari contingeret, ex quo benedictionis tota effluxit ubertas? Non modo staret et exsiccaretur fluxus sanguinis sed statim emanaret impetus fluminis, illius utique qui laetificat civitatem Dei.*

3. Felix, inquam, haec mulier et multum felix quae tetigit fimbriam, sed excellentius felix, quae amplius aliquid ausa gloriatur et dicit: 'fasciculus myrrhae dilectus meus mihi; in medio uberum meorum commorabitur'.* Talem sponsa frequenter experta complexum, elapsum rursus anxius quaerit. Audi quid loquitur: 'in lectulo meo per noctem quaesivi, quem diligit anima mea'.* Vide quomodo et locus et tempus negotio competit. 'In lectulo', inquit, 'meo quaesivi'; ibi enim potest investigari quietius, inveniri citius et tutius teneri.* Quid ergo est aliud 'in lectulo' nisi in loco secreto et quieto? Jure illic,

for going into hiding, for these are her words: 'in my bed by night I sought him and did not find him'.* It is pleasant enough to seek you, good Jesus, more pleasant to hold you; to seek is the task of devotion, to hold is the fulness of joy. For if healing came to the woman who furtively touched the hem of your garment, what will take place in one who holds and embraces your substance! The crowd was pressing in upon you but she alone kept touching you, perhaps because the crowd rushed in riotously, while the woman approached soberly and silently. She touched you not yet from in front but from behind and the flow of blood was staunched. There stopped in her all the flow of carnal licentiousness, of carnal pleasure and anxiety; all that in her was once fluid and dissolute and wanton, was dammed and dried up, and all this at a touch of the hem of your garment. Full of blessings is the hem of his garment, for ointment falls and flows from his head to the hem of his garment.* Therefore myrrh and a drop [of aloes flows] from your garments,* myrrh indeed from your garments but prize myrrh from your lips, for your lips are lilies distilling prize myrrh.* If there was so much grace in the touch of the hem of his garment, what might have happened had she touched his very head from which has flowed the full bounty of his blessings! Not only would the flow have been staunched and the blood congealed, but straightway there would have been an overflow of that gushing stream which surely gladdens the city of God.*

Sg 3:1; S 1:2, M 13A.

Ps 132:2
Ps 44:9

Sg 5:13

Ps 45:5

3. Happy is this woman, I say very happy in touching the hem of his garment, but surpassing happy is the bride who boasts of having dared something more: 'a sachet of myrrh is my beloved to me that lies between my breasts'.* Having frequenlty experienced such an embrace, again she anxiously seeks him when he has slipped away. Hear what she says: 'Upon my little bed by night I sought him whom my soul loves'.* See how the time and the place are apt for their meeting. 'In my little bed', she says, 'I sought him', for there he can be traced more quietly, found more quickly and held more

Sg 1:12

Sg 3:1

bone Jesu, quaereris, ubi libentius moraris. 'Factus est in pace locus' tuus, 'in pace locus' tuus 'et habitatio in Sion',* hoc est in pace et in speculatione. Praecedit pax, ut speculatio sequatur; 'pacem', inquit apostolus, 'sequamini', 'sine qua nemo videbit Deum'.* Jure ergo quietis delegit locum, quam amor ad quaerendum urgebat ardentior. Denique post curas cum quieti fuerimus redditi, acriorem sentimus morsum amoris divini.* Stupidum enim et insensibilem animum adversus huiusmodi stimulos mundi frequens cura solet efficere; idcirco dicit: 'in lectulo meo quaesivi quem diligit anima mea'. In loco certe brevi, immensum quaesivi, sed novit ipse breviorem se contrahere in modum et contemperare capacitati nostrae.

<blockquote>Ps 75:3

Hebr 12:14

Jos 22:4</blockquote>

4. 'Quaesivi illum in lectulo meo'; mallem in suo, in illo amplo et intimo et occulto recessu et sinu Patris. Beatius plane ipsum penes seipsum cernerem, quem apud me quaererem; ibi enim in veritate et luce, hic in umbra et imagine, et ideo in nocte. 'Per noctem'. inquit, 'quaesivi.' 'In lectulo et per noctem quaesivi', ut habeam aliquem tactum dulcedinis etsi nondum luminis serenum. Potest enim hic dilectus magis suaviter sentiri, quam ad liquidum sciri; 'videmus nunc per speculum et in aenigmate', et quasi 'in nocte'.* Quod si per noctem est quod videmus, quanto magis quod quaerimus! Jure quidem, ubi lux quaeritur, nox commemoratur; neque enim posset lucem tenere et noctem tolerare. Bona tamen nox, quia tempus quietis, tempus absconsionis, tempus amoris aptum negotio. 'Abscondes eos in abscondito faciei tuae, a perturbatione hominum.'* 'Turbatus est', inquit, in via 'oculus meus.'* Bona huius ergo absconsio, quae dum a perturbatione protegit, purgat oculum, fovet aspectum et mentis aciem ad lucem praeparat.

<blockquote>1 Cor 13:12

Ps 30:21
Ps 6:6; Vulg. a furore</blockquote>

securely.* What then is the meaning of 'in my little bed', but in a hidden and quiet place? Rightly are you sought there, good Jesus, where you dally more deliberately. 'His abode has been established in peace and his dwelling in Sion',* that is in peace and in contemplation. Peace precedes, that contemplation may follow; 'strive for peace', says the apostle, 'without which no one will see God'.* Rightly then has she chosen an abode of quiet, for a more ardent love was urging her to seek. After anxieties, when we have been restored to quiet as Scripture says,* we feel a sharper sting of divine love. Frequent cares of the world are wont to make the spirit dull and insensitive to such goads; therefore the bride says: 'in my little bed I sought him whom my soul loves'. Surely in a limited abode I sought the unlimited, but he knows how to limit himself to a smaller measure and to adjust to our capacity.

4. 'I sought him in my little bed', though my preference is for his, in that spacious, intimate and hidden retreat in the bosom of the Father. Yes I would have a more blessed vision of him in his home, whom I am seeking in mine, for there I would see in truth and in light but here in shadow and in a likeness, and therefore in night. 'By night I sought him', says the bride. 'In my little bed and by night I sought him', that I might have some touch of sweetness though not yet the brilliance of light. Here indeed the Beloved can be experienced sweetly rather than known transparently; 'now we see in a mirror dimly', and as it were by night.* But if what we see is in the night, how much more what we seek! Rightly then is the night mentioned when the light is being sought, for one cannot both hold the light and endure the night. Yet the night is good both as a time of quiet and a time of hiding, a time suited to the exchange of love. 'In the covert of your presence you will hide them from the disquiet of men.'* Again the psalmist says: 'my eye was troubled' on the way.* Good is the concealment of the bride, for while protecting her from disquiet, it purifies her

S 1:2, M 13CD

Ps 75:3

Heb 12:14

Jos 22:4

1 Co 13:12

Ps 30:21

Ps 6:8

5. *Melior talis nox die, sed illo de quo propheta: 'diem hominis non concupivi, tu scis'.* Nescio quo pacto sibi adversantur et alterutro se·obscurant dies Domini et dies hominis, si quidem dum alter exoritur, alter reconditur.* 'Diem', inquit, 'hominis non concupivi', hoc est, humanum favorem, hominum gloriam, et inter reliquos, immo prae reliquis spectabilis videri.* Recte hunc diem propheta abjurat, qui perturbationis ministrat materiam.* Melior ergo haec nox die, si quidem nox a perturbatione abscondit, dies exponit. Denique primi parentes nostri, statim ut eorum oculi in hanc aperti sunt lucem, erubescentes confundebantur.* Nos quidem vereor, ne simila et forte ampliora passi, tali modo apertis oculis, caecatis animis, similiter* confundamur, non similiter erubescamus.* Quanto felicius clausa prius tenuere lumina et meliore cooperta nocte,* peccati nescientes pruriginem. Abinde sumpsit hic malus dies originem, qui vitiorum denudavit semitas, illicientes demonstravit species, concupiscentiae oculo sollicitantem ingessit materiam.**

Jer 17:16; Vulg. *desideravi*

S 1:4, M 14CD

3 Reg 17:17
B: *que*

Gen 3:7

B: *simi liciter*
B: *simi liciter*
B: *meliori*

S 1:4, M 15A.

6. *Heu me! quomodo me circumfulget dies ista! quomodo affectum ad se meum abripuit; quomodo claro versantur in lumine ante mentis, oculos et quidem satis importune, impacata simul et impudica! Nusquam fere declinandi, nusquam delitescendi copia, nullae satis tutae sunt latebrae, ita ubique erumpunt et emergunt in cogitatum cuncta quae spiritum vel turbent vel turpent, sive diligenter attrectata, sive leviter tacta. Licet enim animus castigatiore repellat illa proposito, solo tamen sordidatur attactu, quo vel illa tangit vel tangitur ab illis. 'Qui tetigit picem, inquinabitur ab illa.'* Denique secundum legis scita, quarundam rerum tenuis etiam inquinat attactus, licet non ad culpam, ad aliquam tamen affectatae iniuriam munditiae.* Quid cum se contemplanti animo corporeae offundunt imagines, non quae carnalem appetitum provocent, sed quae spiritualem*

Eccli 13:1

Lev 4:8

sight, and prepares the eye of her mind for the light.

5. Such a night is better than the day, but that day of which the prophet speaks: 'the day of man I have not desired, as you know'.* Somehow the day of the Lord and the day of man are opposed to each other, for when one dawns the other fades away. 'I have not desired the day of man', says the prophet, that is the applause of men, human glory, to be respected among others, even above others. Rightly the prophet renounces this day, because it provides a source of disquiet. This night is better than day, since night conceals a man from the disquiet to which the day exposes him. In Genesis, as soon as our first parents opened their eyes to this daylight, they blushed in confusion.* Yet I fear lest after similar or perhaps wider experiences, with eyes equally open but with closed minds, we may match them in confusion but match them in blushing for shame. How much happier were they pre-previously when they kept their eyes closed and when under cover of a better night they knew not sin's concupiscence. Thence this evil day drew its origin, for it laid bare the paths of vice, exposed alluring shapes and presented fascinating objects to the eye of concupiscence.*

Jr 17:16; S 1:4, M 14CD

Gn 3:7

S 1:4, M 15A.

6. Alas, how this day glitters around me, how it ensnared my affections! In what a naked light and how importunately do wild and wanton images together parade before the eyes of the mind! There is practically nowhere to turn aside, nowhere to hide; no hiding place is secure enough. From all sides there break and emerge into consciousness, whether deliberately welcomed or lightly brushed aside, all the images which trouble and defile the spirit. Though with stricter resolution the spirit may repel these images, still the spirit is sullied by the mere contact by which it either touches or is touched by them. 'Whoever touches pitch, will be defiled by it.'* According to the statutes of the Law, even the slightest contact with some objects causes defilement,* although not to our guilt, still with some harm to the purity we profess. What results when

Si 13:1

Lv 4:8

S 1:4, M 15A

B: *avertitur*

S 1:5, M 15BC

Ps 30:21

contuitum tardent?* Nonne melius huiusmodi omnia obscurari quam illustrari? caeca obvolvi caligine quam clara et memori depromi in luce? Bona ergo nox, quae prudenti oblivione dissimulat et avertit* cuncta temporalia ad illum qui aeternus est quarendum tempus expediens et explicans occasiones, quae mundi concupiscentiam abscondit, curam, cogitatum.* Hoc est enim mundum habere absconditum, vel mundo abscondi. Sic etiam abscondi poterimus in abscondito faciei tuae, Domine,* non dico plena notione, sed tamen tota devotione et libera investigatione et aliquanta inventione. Hanc absconsionem, hoc secretum, has latebras quibus mundani diei declinamus vel amorem vel imaginationem, quibus humanum diem aut ablatum non repetimus aut oblatum respuimus, noctis nomine appelari nunc a sponsa crediderim.

Cant 2:3

S 1:5, M 15D

B: *nichil*

Joan 3:20

7. Denique in superioribus dicit: 'sub umbra eius quem desideraveram sedi, et fructus eius dulcis gutturi meo'.* Fructus iste suaviter pascit, si tamen prius umbra protraxerit. Bona umbra, quae carnis prudentiam obscurat et concupiscentiam refigerat. Intelligis quae sit umbra? Inde tibi refulget occasio quomodo et hic noctem intelligas, nisi quod quaedam occultiores latebrae et magis abditae, et accomodatae magis ad investigationis et contemplationis usum, sub noctis exprimuntur quam sub umbrae vocabulo. In umbra, rerum visibilium oblivionem aliquantam accipe, in nocte omnimodam.* Hac ergo ratione, sponsa per noctem se quaerere dicit, quae reliqua iniusta nec respicit nec nota reputat, dum illum quem diligit intenta suspirat. Sed nos, fratres, quid in lectulo, quid per noctem, id est, quid in nostro vel occulto vel otio quaerimus? Utinam nihil* earum quae pudore magis quam praedicatione digna sint, et operiri quam aperiri malint. Qui enim male agit, odit lucem,* et quae in occulto aguntur, turpe est

images of the body pour into a contemplative spirit? Perhaps they do not arouse carnal desires but they do impede spiritual vision. Would not everything of the kind be better concealed than illustrated, better shrouded in an unseeing fog of oblivion than brought into the clear light of remembrance? Good then is the night, which in discreet forgetfulness disguises and turns aside all things temporal, scheduling a time and providing opportunities to seek that day which is eternal!* Good is the night, which hides the concupiscence, the care and the thought of the world. This is indeed to keep the world hidden or to be hidden from the world. We also can be so concealed 'in the covert of your presence',* O Lord, I do not say with full knowledge but with all devotion and free enquiry and some discovery. Our withdrawal, our concealment, our hiding places, whereby we shun either the love or the fancy of worldly daylight, whereby we do not retrieve the world's day once abandoned and scorn the world's day when proffered, these in my opinion are here termed night by the bride.

S 1:5, M 15BC

Ps 30:21

7. In an earlier verse the bride says: 'I sat beneath the shadow of him whom I desired and his fruit was sweet to my palate'.* His fruit gives tasty nourishment, provided his shadow has previously given cover. Good is the shadow which conceals the prudence of the flesh and chills concupiscence. Do you understand the meaning of shadow? The passage on the shadow offers you a brilliant opportunity to understand our passage about night, except that some hiding places, better screened and camouflaged, more suited to the exercise of enquiry and contemplation, are expressed by the word 'night' rather than by 'shadow'. By the word 'shadow' understand some forgetfulness of the visible world and by the word 'night' total oblivion.* For this reason the bride says she seeks him by night, because she neither regards nor acknowledges the rest of the world, while she earnestly sighs for the one she loves. But what do we seek, my brothers, in our little bed and by night, that is, in our hiding place and our leisure? Hopefully,

Sg 2:3

S 1:5, M 15D

Eph 5:12	*et dicere.* Haec vero quaesivit speciosum forma prae filiis hominum; ideo gloriatur et dicit: 'in lectulo meo*
Cant 3:1	*per noctes quaesivi, quem diligit anima mea'.**

	8. *Putas autem quod mysterio vacet hoc ipsum*
S 2:1, M 17D	*quod dicit: 'in lectulo' et non 'in lecto'?* Ego quidem crediderim quia noluit illud sibi exprobrari, quod per prophetam a Domino dicitur: 'dilatasti stratum tuum*
Is 57:8; here Ra: resumes	*iuxta me; suscepisti adulterum'.* Nos ergo non dilatemus sed magis contrahamus stratum conscientiae, cordis lectulum, et illud propheticum merito nobis coaptabitur: 'coangustatum est stratum ut alter decidat, et pallium breve utrumque operire non*
Is 28:20	*potest'.* Breve enim et angustum est cor hominis ad concipiendas vitales divini verbi delicias, etiam cum*
S 2:1, M 18A Ra: *illas in totum*	*in illas totum extenditur, nedum ad alia distentum.* Et ut ad simile vos provocem exemplum,*
BRa: *nichil*	*nihil* a vobis, fratres, vel studiose quaeratur vel desidiosis ingeratur, quod sponsi offendat praesentiam, confundat conscientiam, conscientiam dico*
1 Cor 10:29	*vestram, neque alterius.**

	9. *Illud quoque observandum, quod dicit 'in lectulo meo'. Alibi enim legis communiter dictum:*
Cant 1:15	*'lectulus noster floridus'.* Forsitan est aliquis qui*
S 2:4-5, M 19B-20C	*solius sponsi sit lectulus.* Quis vero iste erit, nisi alta illa et intima quies divinae bonitatis et sapientiae,*
Ra: omits *sacratum*	*illud aeternum tranquillitatis secretum et sacratum silentium, totiusque*. Trinitatis unitas et pax, 'quae*
Phil 4:7	*exsuperat omnem sensum!'* Et quidem 'multae*
Joan 14:2	*mansiones in domo Patris mei sunt';* Ipse vero*
1 Tim 6:16	*lucem habitat inaccessibilem;* denique summus ponti-*
Lev 16:17, Heb 9:7 *Matth 11:27 †B: *patrem?* Ra: *patrem.*	*fex sancta sanctorum solus ingreditur.* Et 'Patrem nemo novit nisi Filius et cui ipse voluerit revelare'.* Quod ergo paternum† novit Filius sicut ipse novit, solius ipsius est et ceteris incommunicabile. Quan-*

nothing which deserves shame rather than acclaim, which prefers to be concealed rather than revealed. For one 'who does evil, hates the light',* and deeds done in the dark 'it is shameful even to mention'.* But the bride sought the 'fairest in form among the sons of men'.* Therefore she boasts and says: 'in my little bed by night I sought him whom my soul loves'.* *Jo 3:20*
Ep 5:12

Ps 44:3
Sg 3:1

8. Do you think her use of the diminutive is without hidden meaning, when she says 'in a little bed' and not 'in a bed'?* Personally I would suppose that she was unwilling to bear the reproach spoken by the Lord through the prophet: 'you have spread wide your couch beside me; you have welcomed an adulterer'.* Therefore let us not widen but rather narrow the couch of our conscience, the little bed of our heart. Then the verse of the prophet will be rightly applied to us: 'the couch is so narrow that the one or the other may fall out, and the short blanket cannot cover both'.* Indeed the heart of man is confined and narrow in welcoming the living delights of God's word, even when man's heart is wide open for those delights and far from being open to other delights. To challenge you to emulate her example, let nothing be earnestly sought by you, brothers, or undertaken among the idle, which might offend the presence of the Bridegroom or confound one's conscience, 'I mean your own, not the conscience of another'.*

S 2:1, M 17D

Is 57:8

Is 28:20; S 2:1, M 18A.

1 Co 10:29

9. The pronoun she uses should also be noticed, 'in my little bed'.* Elsewhere you read of a shared bed; 'our little bed is all flowers'.* Perhaps there is a little bed reserved for the Bridegroom alone. But what will this be, if not that deep and intimate quiet of the divine goodness and wisdom, that eternal, secret and sacred silence of tranquillity, the unity and peace of the whole Trinity 'which surpasses all understanding'.* Yes indeed, 'in my Father's home there are many rooms',* but he 'dwells in unapproachable light',* and the high priest enters the holy of holies alone.* 'And no one knows the Father except the Son and anyone to whom the Son wishes to reveal him.'* What the Son knows about the

S 2:4-5, M 19B-20C.
*Sg 1:15

Ph 4:7
Jo 14:2
1 Tm 6:16
Lv 16:17, Heb 9:7

Mt 11:27

tum nobis revelare dignatur, in secreti nos sui cubiculum ex parte admittit, et quietis suae communicat lectulum.

10. *Illum vero quem suum sponsa lectulum vocat, vide si non recte rationalis animae possit accipi natura; huius enim divinae essentiae in se obtinet imaginem, sed non veritatem. Cum ergo ex propriae consideratione naturae divinam vel quaerit vel contemplatur substantiam, ut in umbra et imagine veritatem inveniat, tunc istud dicere non incongrue poterit, de quo nunc agitur: 'in lectulo meo per* Ra: *noctesque* *noctes* quaero quem diligit anima mea'. 'Quem diligit', inquit, non 'quem metuit', semper enim quem timemus horremus, quem amamus optamus, nec possumus eius optare praesentiam, cuius formidamus sententiam. Dilectio vero super meritum extendit votum; immo idem illi est, votum et meritum, 'finis enim praecepti caritas de corde puro et conscientia* 1 Tim 1:5 *bona'.* Nescit caritas bona carere conscientia, si* 1 Cor 13:4 *quidem caritas nihil perperam agit,* et quae per-* 1 Petr 4:8 *peram gesta sunt, operit.* Nil bona tutius conscientia: bona conscientia audet et caritas ardet; illa non formidat, ista inflammat; illa pro delicto* S 1:7, M 16CD *non confundit, ista super dilecto confidit.* Magna vis amoris: alieno non nititur suffragio, propriis contenta meritis; semper amari se praesumit, quae amara se sentit; denique, non respectis aliis maiestatis nominibus, solum sponsa dilectum memo-* Ra: *nominat et* *rat,* quae singulariter intus tolerat aestus amoris.* memorat *Hoc autem attendendum, quam* frequenter dilecti* *Ra: *quod* †S 1:8, M 17A *recenset vocabulum,† quocumque ex mysterio: 'dilec-* Cant 5:10 *tus meus candidus et rubicundus',* et 'talis est* Cant 5:16 *dilectus meus',* et in praesenti, 'quem diligit anima* Cant 3:1 *mea'.* Magna certe sermonis huius gratia, nec mirum si frequentatur in ore, quod fervet in corde. Ideo et animam commemorat, non enim verbo tantum diligit* S 1:7, M 17A *sed voto, nec solo actu sed magis affectu.**

Father, then, exactly as the Son knows, belongs to the Son alone and is incommunicable to others. As far as the Son thinks fit to make a revelation to us, he admits us partially into the chamber of his hiding place and shares the little bed of his repose.

10. But consider whether the little bed which the bride calls her own, might not rightly be understood as the nature of the rational soul, for it contains in itself the image though not the reality of his divine essence. When therefore from a consideration of its own nature, the soul seeks or contemplates the divine substance, in order to discover the divine reality in its shadow and image, the soul will then be able to utter without inconsistency the verse we are discussing: 'in my little bed by night I seek him whom my soul loves'. 'Whom my soul loves', are her words, not 'whom my soul fears', for we always shun the one we fear but long for the one we love, nor can we long for the presence of one whose judgment we dread. Perfect love indeed extends its longing beyond its merit, or rather, for perfect love longing and merit are the same thing, for 'the aim of our charge is charity arising from a pure heart and a good conscience'.* Charity presupposes the presence of a good conscience, since charity does nothing falsely,* and charity covers what has been done falsely.* Nothing is more secure than a good conscience.* A good conscience is bold for its love is not cold; it lives without fright for love sets it alight; it does not blush for a fault for love trusts the Beloved. Great is the power of love. Love does not rely on another's favor but is satisfied with its own deserts. Conscious that it loves, it assumes that it is always loved. In the Canticle, disregarding his other titles of distinction, the bride mentions only her 'Beloved', because in a special way she endures within, the ardor of his love. Notice how frequently, whatever the mystery, she recalls the word 'Beloved';* 'my Beloved is radiant and ruddy',* and 'such is my Beloved',** and in the present verse, 'whom my soul loves'.* Great surely is the charm of this word. It is no surprise if what glows in her heart overflows from her lips. For this reason

1 Tm 1:5
1 Co 13:4
1 P 4:8
S 1:7, M 16CD

S 1:8, M 17A.
*Sg 5:10
**Sg 5:16
*Sg 3:1

11. Quid vero sibi vult, quod 'animam', non 'spiritum' dicit? Forte quia dilecto quem adhuc quaerebat, nondum adhaerebat, 'qui enim adhaeret Domino,* unus est spiritus'.** Et quidem nusquam in toto hoc cantico spiritum nominat, sed 'anima mea liquefacta est',* et 'anima mea conturbavit me',* et hoc ipsum frequenter: 'quem diligit anima mea',* id quoque fere nusquam nisi cum absentem quaerit, vel abesse queritur. Solent his nominibus gradus quidam distingui animae perfectioris et minus perfectae. Apostolus dicit: 'animalis homo non percipit quae sunt spiritus Dei'.* Ego animam hanc ita amantem et aestuantem, ferventem et quaerentem, nunquam non spiritualem dixerim, quippe quae licet nondum plena visione, voto tamen propenso illi adhaerebat, quem vehementer diligebat.*

Ra: Deo et Domino
**1 Cor 6:17

Cant 5:6
Cant 6:11
Cant 3:1

1 Cor 2:14

S 1:8, M 17BC

12. Possumus autem non incongrue, sicut in spiritu, subtilem et attenuatum intellectum, sic in anima, suavem et tenerum accipere affectum. Per prophetam in promissione Dominus dicit: 'dabo vobis cor carneum';* si ergo carnis nomen in bono alicubi accipitur, cur non magis animae? Ego beatam hanc animam, ut licenter loquar, non corneam sed carneam magis iudicaverim, et nil habentem in se rigoris vel duritae, sed mollem, teneram, tractabilem et sensibilem ad singulos divini verbi aculeos, denique ut dicat: 'neque caro mea aenea est,'* sed quam spiritualis pertranseat gladius,* et caritate se vulneratam gaudeat. Sagittae eius acutae sunt,* et leniter illabuntur animo, et sine laesione ad intima penetrant, et statum mentis inebriant, et in quosdam inexpertos et insperatos commutant affectus, nisi quod caritas 'omnia sperat',* et eorum quae iam percepit argumento, maiora sibi pollicetur.

Ez 11:19

Job 6:12
Luc 2:35
Ps 44:6

1 Cor 13:7

also she refers to her soul, for she loves not only in word but also in her heart, not in deed alone but especially in affection.

11. Now what is meant by her mention of 'soul' rather than 'spirit'? Perhaps because she did not yet cling to her Beloved whom she was still seeking, for 'he who clings to the Lord is one spirit with him'.* Indeed nowhere in the entire Canticle does she mention the word 'spirit', but she says, 'my soul melted',* and 'my soul was troubled',** and frequently as in the present verse, 'he whom my soul loves'.* Even this verse she almost never uses except when she seeks him in his absence or complains of his absence. By these terms several degrees of perfection are usually distinguished: a soul more perfect and a soul less perfect. The apostle says: 'an unspiritual man does not receive the gifts of the Spirit of God'.* Personally I would never call unspiritual, this soul so ardently in love and so fervent in her quest, for although still without full vision yet with ever increasing desire she clings to him whom she passionately loves.

1 Co 6:17

Sg 5:6
**Sg 6:11*
Sg 3:1

1 Co 2:14, S:18, M 17BC.

12. As we can aptly consider 'spirit' to mean a subtle and refined understanding, so we can consider 'soul' to mean a gentle and tender affection. The Lord promises us through the prophet: 'I will give you a heart of flesh'.* If then in some passage, the word 'flesh' is understood in a good sense, why not still more the word 'soul'? If I may speak freely, I would personally consider this blessed soul not one of horn but rather of flesh, having nothing stubborn or harsh but being soft, tender, pliable and sensitive to every dart from the divine Word, so that with Job it may say 'not of bronze is my flesh',* but flesh which the sword of the spirit may pierce,* and which may rejoice in having been wounded by charity. The arrows of the word are sharp,* and slip gently into the spirit, without mortal wound penetrate to its depths, change the mind to a state of inebriation and transform it with affections beyond experience and expectation, except that 'charity hopes for all things',* and on the strength of what charity already

Esk 11:19

Jb 6:12
Lk 2:35

Ps 44:6

1 Co 13:7

13. *Felix plane cor, in quo omnis emollita est duritia et rigor et insensibilitas, spiritus calefacta et animata alloquio, ignitum enim eloquium eius vehementer,* et 'molliti sunt sermones eius super oleum, et ipsi sunt jacula'.* 'Oleum', inquit, et 'jacula', perungunt enim et compungunt, sauciant et sanant, instigant et mitigant; mitigant tumorem, instigant ad amorem. Oleum sunt, dum sensim et non sine mora intrant in interiora; jacula vero, propter amoris impetum et impatientiam desiderii anxie concupiscentis et aegre carentis. Oleum quia leniter et lente mentem inficit; jaculum, quia transitorio sed intolerabili amoris ictu sentientem consumit paene et conficit. In oleo, dulcis et diuturnior sensus; in jaculo, vehemens sed velox excessus. Propter huiusmodi animam dicit quia sit spiritualis amoris succensa igniculo, saucia jaculo, fota oleo, informata eloquio.*

Ps 118:140
Ps 54:22

SUPER HESTERNO CAPITULO

14. *Super hesterno capitulo, hodernum vobis instauramus convivium, nec enim ibi cuncta dicta sunt quae dicenda occurrunt.* Et primo non satis admirari possum de ipsa clausularum serie et consequentiae rerum.* Quae enim ordinis ratio, ut sponsa tam dilecta, tam docta, quaerat in lectulo quem salientem proxime reliquit in montibus, quaerat in plateis quem pascentem proponit in liliis?* Stupenda plane ratio, ut inter angustias requirat lectuli, qui libertate montium, caprearum levitate vaga perfruitur! Si figuris istis spiritualium proponitur series et ordo profectuum, valde quidem reconditus est, affectum vero varietas manifesta. Ubi profectus docetur tenor quidam et gradata servatur dispositio; ubi loquitur affectus et amor, libera passim lege vagatur, et quod prius*

S 2:1, M 17C

S 1:1, M 11A

Cant 2:16-17

perceives, promises itself still greater gifts.

13. Obviously happy is the heart, in which has been softened all harshness and stubbornness and insensitivity, after being warmed and enlivened by the exhortation of the spirit whose eloquence burns with passion,* and whose 'words are softer than oil although they are arrows'.* His words are 'oil' and 'arrows' says the psalmist, for they are both unction and compunction, they cut and they cure, they are a spur and a bridle, a bridle for our pride and a spur for our love. They are oil when gently and without haste they seep into our interior, but they are arrows no less, thanks to the impetuosity of love and the impatience of longing, when the lover fondly frets and grows wan with waiting. Yes they are oil, because imperceptibly and slowly they penetrate the mind, but arrows because with the transient and intolerable wound of love they almost devour and destroy their victim. In oil there is a sweet and more lasting experience, in arrows a fiery but fleeting ecstasy.* Thanks to a soul of this kind, the bride says she is aflame with an ember of spiritual love, wounded by an arrow, soothed with oil and formed by eloquence.

Ps 118:140
Ps 54:22

G. avoids ecstasis

SUPER HESTERNO CAPITULO

14. From yesterday's passage let me celebrate with you the banquet of today.³ First, I cannot sufficiently wonder at the very series of the clauses and the sequence of events. What is the explanation of this order, that the bride, so beloved and so experienced, should seek in her little bed for one whom she recently left leaping upon the mountains,* and that she should seek in the squares for one she envisions grazing among lilies?* Obviously amazing is the explanation of why she seeks within the confines of her little bed for one who enjoys the freedom of the mountains and the carefree nimbleness of gazelles. If in these figures a sequence and order of spiritual progress is envisioned, it is well hidden indeed, though the variety of the bride's affections is mani-

Sg 2:17
Sg 2:16

erumpit in animum, eructat in canticum. Non est autem nunc nostri vel otii vel ingenii, omnes carminis huius clausulas consequentem et evidentem summatim digerere in seriem. Propterea relicta hac communi summa, redeamus ad singula.

Prov 15:15 S 2:2, M 18BC	15. 'In lectulo meo per noctes quaesivi.' Bonus plane lectulus de quo legis in proberbiis: 'secura mens quasi juge convivium';* foris nox, foris turbatio, sed tranquillitas intus, quasi quietis lectulus quidam.* Non est hic illud lamentabile dicere: 'foris interficit
Lam 1:20	gladius et domi mors similis est'.* Immo si foris gladius, intus gaudium: 'spe', inquit, 'gaudentes,
Rom 12:12	in tribulatione patientes'.* Ad noctem tribulatio refertur, ad lectulum spes et gaudium. Forte propter hoc non lectum sed lectulum parco appellat vocabulo, quoniam totum gaudium nostrum fere in spe est ad-
S 2:2, M 18C	huc et ex parte.*²

fest. When some sequence of events in perfect harmony is being explained, then step by step the order of events is maintained; but when affection and love is the singer, then the tune wanders here and there with a law of its own, and what first breaks in upon the spirit, bursts into song. Now however, it is beyond either my leisure or my talent, to arrange by way of summary all the clauses of this Canticle into an orderly and obvious sequence. Therefore abandoning a general summary, let us return to the individual clauses of the Canticle.

15. 'In my little bed by night I sought him.'* *Sg 3:1, S 2:2, M 18BC.* Good obviously is the little bed of which you read in Proverbs: 'a carefree mind is a perpetual feast';* *Pr 15:15* outside is the night, outside the hurricane, but inside is tranquillity like a little bed of repose. Here there is no need to repeat the lament: 'outside the sword slays and indoors is like a death'.* Rather, if outside *Lm 1:20* is the sword, inside is rejoicing, 'rejoicing in hope', says the apostle, 'patient under tribulation'.* Tribula- *Rm 12:12* tion is attributed to the night, hope and rejoicing to the little bed. Perhaps for this reason the bride says not 'a bed', but 'a little bed', the diminutive term, because practically all our rejoicing is still in hope and imperfect.[4]

NOTES ON *MIRA SIMPLICITAS*

1. Bodleian Ms 24, of the 12th-13th century, contains G.'s Epistles, *Epistolae Gilleberti Quondam Abbatis Hoylandiae*, his *Tractatus*, and his incomplete *Sermo* on the sower, and immediately following in the same first hand, ff. 96v-106v, beginning *Mira simplicitas*, is what Jean Leclercq considered perhaps a first draft of the *Sermones* as finally printed; see 'La première rédaction des *Sermones in Cantica* de Gilbert de Hoyland', RB 62 (1952) 289-90, and Mikkers 272. In the first *Sermones* as finally printed, G. changed the emphasis from *simplicitas* to *affectus amantium*, but he returned frequently to *simplicitas* later: S16:5, 22:3, 5, 41:1, 43:3. Here, apparently in a first printing in any language of *Mira simplicitas*, references are given to the *Sermones* where many sentences are identical, and an enumeration of paragraphs has been added for convenient reference.

2. De Lubac I:603, nn. 2-3, lists early authors who mention the nut and the honeycomb to distinguish the literal and the spiritual senses of scripture; some of these authors may have been familiar to Gilbert, Origen for example in the translation of Rufinus. G. does not mention the nut elsewhere nor the honeycomb in this meaning, though he returns to the honeycomb elsewhere at length: Ep 2:2-3, T 4:3-5, S 41:3-7, where he comments on Sg 4:11 and 5:1. He is obviously thinking of Pr 16:24, 'favus mellis composita verba', and Pr 24:13, where wisdom is 'favum dulcissimum gutturi tuo' and perhaps Lk 24:42. See my article, 'The Honeycomb in Gilbert of Hoyland' in CSt 14 (1979).

3. S 2:1, M 17C. The first letter is capitalized as if to begin a second sermon.

4. The text of *Mira simplicitas* ends here.

www.ingramcontent.com/pod-product-compliance
Lightning Source LLC
Chambersburg PA
CBHW020649300426
44112CB00007B/306